Savoring God

Savoring God

praying with all our senses

Kathleen Finley

ave maria press   Notre Dame, Indiana

© 2003 by Ave Maria Press, Inc.

www.avemariapress.com

International Standard Book Number: 0-87793-981-0

Cover and text design by Brian C. Conley

Printed and bound in the United States of America.

Library of Congress Cataloging-in-Publication Data
Finley, Kathleen.
  Savoring God : praying with all our senses / Kathleen Finley.
    p. cm.
  Includes bibliographical references.
  ISBN 0-87793-981-0 (pbk.)
  1. Prayer--Christianity. I. Title.
BV210.3 F555 2003
248.3'2--dc21
                                                          2002014342
                                                          CIP

THIS BOOK IS FOR THE WOMEN OF WHISPR,
WHO HAVE SHARED WITH AND TAUGHT ME SO MUCH
ABOUT PRAYER AND SPIRITUALITY.

Contents

Introduction

Our Senses Are
There for a Reason

Fasten your spiritual seat belt. This book is an invitation to a different way of praying—and to a different way of seeing.

Usually when we pray we try to shut out the outside world and focus on the interior, the spiritual, the realm that we often think of as beyond or above us—the transcendent—in order to be able to be with God. Instead, this book invites you to be with God *through* the very tangible, specific objects of your everyday life, to take another look—as well as another listen, taste, touch, and smell—at what is right before you and to see God there. God has given us our five senses as important ways to understand and appreciate the world around us; this is an opportunity to use them specifically for prayer.

The Hebrew and Christian scriptures remind us that in Jesus our God is a God-with-us, Emmanuel. Christians believe that Jesus was, and is, God incarnate or, as a wonderful young theologian-to-be put it, "God's show-and-tell." In Jesus *all* of human life and creation has become a sign of God's presence, filled with sacraments with a small "S," with ways to grow closer to God if we just look again—re-spect—what is right before us.

Jesus was very aware of our senses and spent much of his ministry healing the senses of those who came to him. When John the Baptist sent some of his followers to ask Jesus whether he was the Messiah, the Chosen One, his response to them was this: "Go and tell John what you have seen and heard: the blind receive their sight, the lame walk, the lepers are cleansed, the deaf hear, the dead are raised, the poor have good news brought to them" (Luke 7:22). We see scene after scene in the gospels where Jesus is healing those who are blind and deaf—and as we hear this good news, each of us, in turn, is invited to see and hear more fully.

However, we're realizing that different people may see and hear in many different ways. We've learned a lot in the past century about different personality types and different learning styles. Whether it's the sixteen Myers-Briggs personality types based on Carl Jung's work or the nine Enneagram numbers or an awareness of the primary ways or styles through which we learn, we are coming to a deeper realization that we don't all do things the same way. This includes praying. In the words of the title of a helpful book by Dr. Charles Keating, *Who We Are Is How We Pray.*

If you see yourself as a hands-on person and learner—someone with what the experts call bodily-kinesthetic intelligence—or someone who has a hard time focusing on a fold-your-hands-and-close-your-eyes type of prayer without becoming distracted, this approach may be for you. However, it's not for everyone.

This is an experiment—or, more properly, a series of experiments—in a different, perhaps more playful, imaginative, and right-brained approach to prayer than you may be used to. It may seem silly at times—who ever heard of praying with keys or underwear? See if this works for you. If it doesn't, keep looking; you'll find a way of prayer that will work well for you. God is eager to "get through" to each one of us and gives us an incredible variety of gifts every day—from sunsets to thunderstorms—to get our attention and to remind us of our Creator's limitless love for each of us.

In our relationship with this gracious God, prayer is a time for us to slow down a bit, focus ourselves, and be with God, to spend time with the Creator as we would with a good friend. To put it informally, prayer is time to "hang out" with God. But often good quality "hanging out"—whether with a friend or with God—may take a bit of planning and clearing the schedule to help it happen. Probably the most difficult part of this or any type of prayer is finding a place and a time for that prayer, so that the rest of life doesn't just take over and monopolize all one's time and energy with busyness.

Plan for ten to fifteen minutes as you begin these prayer exercises; you may want to spend more time later as you get into it. It's good to have a space where you won't be disturbed for that amount of time, whether that means shutting the door to the room where you are, letting the answering machine handle any phone calls, or even putting up a "do not disturb" sign. If that's not possible, maybe you can grab a cup of coffee at the kitchen table while the kids are playing in the other room. It sounds hard to do, but you're worth it! Think of it as finding a quiet space to have a catch-up long-distance call with someone you haven't talked to in a while! (But faith tells us that it's really not that long a distance at all to God!)

There is no particular order to these suggested prayer exercises, except that it's helpful to start with the one using a candle, because we will then use the candle as a focus point in the other exercises. ("Exercises" seems to be the best term for these prayers, since calling them "meditations" seems too formal, and in a way they are like exercises you might do to help increase the strength of your eyesight or hearing or another of the senses.)

After making sure you have on hand what is needed for the particular exercise, sit comfortably—but not *too comfortably*—take a few deep breaths, light the candle as instructed, and begin. (If you don't have a particular object called for in one of the exercises, substitute something that would work for you or skip that particular exercise.) There are several parts to each of these exercises.

The first section is **Centering**, with a suggested prayer to help you recover a sense of God's presence, a presence which we know is always with us but one which we can forget so much of the time. This is the time to prepare ourselves to just "be" with God. Try spreading your hands open during the opening prayer so that you use your body even here. If the written prayer is not helpful to you and you would rather use your own words or a different prayer, please use what works for you.

The second section is **Savoring**, a time to use your senses to explore the particular object in the prayer exercise. When you are touching or looking or using your other senses in the prayer exercise, try to do it as if for the very first time, hungrily, the way an infant or toddler seems to take in information; God wants to come to you through your senses.

Next comes **Listening**, a chance to explore how God's word is connected to this particular object or image and to deepen your perception of the object in light of the Christian tradition. There are several scripture passages given; you may wish to focus on just one of them or to read and savor each one. It is important not to hurry here but to roll God's word around in your head and let it mix with what you're seeing before you and what your other senses have told you. Reading the passage aloud may help your ears to become involved as well as your eyes.

Considering, which is a time to reflect on that object, comes next. This is a time to think about the ways that this object interacts with us in our daily lives, to take what we may know about this object and make the connections to our spirituality.

Last, but certainly not least, is the section called **Responding**. This is an opportunity to explore the implications of our reflection for the rest of our lives, the so-what factor. John Shea once commented that the result of prayer for the Christian is always new action. What difference will this prayer exercise make in my life after I finish it? Is there anything that I will do or see in a new way as a result of this prayer time? This section suggests some possibilities; only you can decide what that might be in your own life. This section ends with a brief prayer and with the word "Amen," an ancient Hebrew word meaning "It is true."

If at all possible, after the prayer exercise, it would be good to leave the object that you prayed with out in a prominent place for a few days as a reminder of your prayer and the need to stay open to God's goodness.

These exercises are just the beginning of what can happen in this approach to prayer; there are many more possibilities to pray with, based on each person's interests and the unique setting of every life. Gardeners, for example, will probably want to pray with some garden tools, teens with symbols of their lives, and those with babies with a diaper and the infant toys that are so much a part of their lives. Those involved with a particular sport can pray with symbols of that sport, and musicians can pray with their instruments, while those with disabilities will want to pray with a symbol of that challenge in their lives. The possibilities are nearly endless.

Hopefully, the result of this kind of prayer for you will be a new way of beginning to taste and see God's presence (or presents) all around you. Blessings to you on your journey of discovery!

> O taste and see that the LORD is good.
>
> —PSALM 34:8

Candle: The Light of Christ

Materials at hand: A favorite candle, scented or unscented, and a match or lighter for it. If possible, do this in a darkened or dimly lit area.

Centering (Suggested Opening Prayer—or your own)
(With hands spread open say:)
Loving God, Creator of all that is,
here I am—today, in this place,
with all the senses you have given me.
Help me to use them to come to experience you more deeply.
You are present everywhere around me;
open me to know more of the many ways
that your goodness surrounds me.
Thank you for this time to be with you and to listen to you.
Amen.

Savoring (Senses at Work)
Look at the unlit candle as it waits to do what it was meant to do: give light. Touch it and sense its texture and shape. Smell it to determine if it has a scent or not.

Now prepare to light it and watch as the candle is slowly transformed into a source of light. Smell the bit of smoke as the wick lights and as the match is blown out, if you are using a match. If we were to use this candle or the source of its flame to light many candles, the light of this one would not be diminished in any way. This light could be magnified many times without diminishing any of the flames it helped "foster."

Hold your hands close enough to the flame to feel the warmth without being burned, and watch how the candle's light changes the appearance of the objects around it as it throws the light that is and is not its own.

Listening (The Word of God)

Listen to and reflect on one or more of these passages as you watch the candle's flame:

> Again Jesus spoke to them, saying, "I am the light of the world. Whoever follows me will never walk in darkness but will have the light of life." (John 8:12)
>
> *
>
> It is you who light my lamp; the LORD, my God, lights up my darkness. (Psalm 18:28)
>
> *
>
> The LORD is my light and my salvation; whom shall I fear? The LORD is the stronghold of my life; of whom shall I be afraid? (Psalm 27:1)
>
> *
>
> "You are the light of the world. A city built on a hill cannot be hid. No one after lighting a lamp puts it under the bushel basket, but on the lampstand, and it gives light to all in the house. In the same way, let your light shine before others, so that they may see your good works and give glory to your Father in heaven." (Matthew 5:14-16)

Considering (Time to Reflect)

Until the last century or so, our only sources of light were candles and lamps of various sorts, apart from sunlight. Although we don't often experience total darkness in our culture, the symbol of light as truth in the midst of the darkness of falsity and fear and evil is still a strong and powerful one.

Our God is the ultimate source of light and truth; St. Paul, for example, experienced Christ's presence at the time of his conversion as a strong light which asked Paul why he was persecuting Christ in the early Christians. This light blinded Paul until he could fully "see" in faith.

Loving God, help me to "see" more clearly how you are the light in my life and to appreciate the ways that you dispel the darkness of my doubts and fears with the strong flame of your love.

Responding (So What?)

In the first Letter of John we read: "Whoever says, 'I am in the light,' while hating a brother or sister, is still in the darkness. Whoever loves a brother or sister lives in the light, and in such a person there is no cause for stumbling" (1 John 2:9-10).

If I am to really live in the light, then I need to realize that God's love and light is there for *everyone* around me, even the person I find it hardest to love right now. (Name a specific person or two for yourself here.)

Loving God and source of all light, help me to bring the light of your love to all whom I meet and work with. Amen.

(We will be using the candle in the other meditations to help us focus on God's presence.)

Praying With Nature

Water: The Source of Life

Materials at hand: A pitcher of water and a bowl (clear, if possible), with a candle as a prayer focus.

Centering

(Light the candle and with your hands spread open say:)
Loving God, Creator of all that is,
here I am—today, in this place,
with all the senses you have given me.
Help me to use them to come to experience you more deeply.
You are present everywhere around me;
open me to know more of the many ways
that your goodness surrounds me.
Thank you for this time to be with you and to listen to you.
Amen.

Savoring

Look at the water inside the pitcher. Sense its stillness and calm as it fills the space inside the pitcher. Listen as you pour it out into the bowl, hearing as you do the rushing of waterfalls, of heavy rains, even of tidal waves. Watch as it settles now into a new "home," becoming at rest within a new space, and watch as the candlelight plays on the surface of the water, picking up the smallest movements.

Now touch the water, scooping it up into your hands, washing your face and taking a drink, if you'd like. This is a very daily action, but how does it feel to do this with renewed awareness? For a moment, in your imagination, be someone in the desert or a plant in very dry soil that has been thirsting for this water for days. Watch a few drops on your finger in the candlelight and see how each one is actually a miniature lens, reflecting all that surrounds it, creating a sort of natural kaleidoscope.

Water is a truly amazing part of our lives.

Listening

Listen to and reflect on one or more of these passages as you watch the candlelight play across the water:

> In the beginning when God created the heavens and the earth, the earth was a formless void and darkness covered the face of the deep, while a wind from God swept over the face of the waters. (Genesis 1:1-2)
>
> *
>
> O God, you are my God, I seek you, my soul thirsts for you; my flesh faints for you, as in a dry and weary land where there is no water. (Psalm 63:1)
>
> *
>
> As a deer longs for flowing streams, so my soul longs for you, O God. My soul thirsts for God, for the living God. When shall I come and behold the face of God? (Psalm 42:1-2)
>
> *
>
> All you who are thirsty, come to the water! (Isaiah 55:1, NAB)

Considering

Our bodies are at least seventy percent water, and we know that water is needed for all life. When we find ourselves rather lifeless or out of energy or ideas, we speak of "running dry." From our beginnings in the watery home of the womb, water is there to quench our thirst, to wash us, to swim in, and to keep our world green.

When we can turn on the faucet and have water whenever we want, it's easy to forget what a gift good old H_2O is. Every once in a while we may get a glimpse of its preciousness at a time of drought or low rainfall, and although other parts of the world may already have been aware of it, we're really just beginning to realize how fragile and prone to pollution our water supply really is.

Responding

There are plenty of ways to refresh my thirst other than with water, even at times when water is really what I need. Sometimes it's even easier to ignore or cover up my true spiritual thirst. Help me to be more aware of how much I long for you in my life, my God—a thirst that I often get too busy to be aware of.

In John's gospel we read:

> Jesus said to [the Samaritan woman], "Everyone who drinks of this water will be thirsty again, but those who drink of the water that I will give them will never be thirsty. The water that I will give will become in them a spring of water gushing up to eternal life." (John 4:13-14)

God of mountain streams and dripping kitchen sinks, help me to realize more deeply my thirst for you, which only you can satisfy. You are, as they say, the Real Thing. And, although an ad might remind me to "accept no substitutes," too often I've settled for what doesn't really "satisfy my thirst" for you.

Please bless those people who help keep our water flowing and clean, and bless those without clean water and those who experience either drought or floods—too little or too much water. And help me remember you the next time I turn on a faucet or a drinking fountain or climb into the shower or the tub. Amen.

Plant or Flower: Growing in Love

Materials at hand: A house plant or cut flower(s), with a candle as a prayer focus.

Centering

(Light the candle and with your hands spread open say:)
Loving God, Creator of all that is,
here I am—today, in this place,
with all the senses you have given me.
Help me to use them to come to experience you more deeply.
You are present everywhere around me;
open me to know more of the many ways
that your goodness surrounds me.
Thank you for this time to be with you and to listen to you.
Amen.

Savoring

As you look at the plant or flower before you, follow the lines of it with your eye, as though you were sketching it and needed to memorize its lines and shape. Notice especially the gracefulness of the leaves and the petals as they attach to the stem(s). Pay attention to the changes in color tones and textures as you observe this plant life before you. Also notice which parts of the plant or flower are especially strong and which are especially delicate and which parts may be a combination of both qualities.

Next use your nose. Closing your eyes to focus on just one sense, smell the plant or flower and take in all that your nose can tell you. Is it what you thought you would smell, or are there some aspects of the scent that you weren't expecting? If you touch or bend the plant slightly, is there a stronger smell? Can you see how the blooms, if there are any, attract not only by their color and pleasing appearance but also by their scent?

Next use your fingers very gently, either with or without your eyes open. Start at the tip of the stem, at a flower or a leaf, and trace your way back to the source of this plant's nourishment, through the stem to the roots—or to the water if it is a cut flower. As you do so, think about the food energy making its way along this route from the roots, giving this plant its energy and life, and about the amazingly complex process that allows this to happen. Notice the variety of textures and surfaces along your "journey," all on the same plant.

Listening

Listen to and reflect on one or more of these passages as you watch the candlelight play across the flower or plant:

So God created humankind . . . . God said [to them], "See, I have given you every plant yielding seed that is upon the face of all the earth, and every tree with seed in its fruit; you shall have them for food. And to every beast of the earth, and to every bird of the air, and to everything that creeps on the earth, everything that has the breath of life, I have given every green plant for food." And it was so. (Genesis 1:27, 29-30)

*

A voice cries out: "In the wilderness prepare the way of the LORD, make straight in the desert a highway for our God." . . . A voice says, "Cry out!" And I said, "What shall I cry?" All people are grass, their constancy is like the flower of the field. The grass withers, the flower fades, when the breath of the LORD blows upon it; surely the people are grass. The grass withers, the flower fades; but the word of our God will stand forever. (Isaiah 40:3, 6-8)

*

The time is surely coming, says the LORD, when . . . I will restore the fortunes of my people Israel, and they shall rebuild the ruined cities and inhabit them; they shall plant vineyards and drink their wine, and they shall make gardens and eat their fruit. I will plant them upon their land, and they shall never again be plucked up out of the land that I have given them, says the LORD your God. (Amos 9:13-15)

*

"Bless the Lord, all that grows in the ground; sing praise to him and highly exalt him forever." (Daniel 3:76)

*

For as the earth brings forth its shoots, and as a garden causes what is sown in it to spring up, so the Lord GOD will cause righteousness and praise to spring up before all the nations. (Isaiah 61:11)

Considering

Plants are far more complex and numerous than they might seem. Scientists estimate that there are about 260,000 species of plants on the earth, from the tiniest mosses to the tallest towering redwoods. We use only a tiny percentage of these species for all the food, shelter, drugs, and fiber that we have today. We depend on plants for so much in our lives, from the photosynthesis which helps give us the air we breathe to the source of most of our foods to the lumber with which to build, even to the fossil fuels that are so essential to our industrial economy, fuels which are the result of the decay of plants now long gone from the earth.

Although they are highly diverse, all plants have three major parts to them: roots, stems, and leaves, each of which is quite complex and uniquely adapted to the environment for that particular variety of plant.

Flowers are the reproductive organs for most plants. Their carefully complex structures are designed not only to give pleasure to the eye through distinctive colors and pigments but also to please the nose through distinctive fragrances due to essential oils in the flower itself. These, in turn, attract insects that can help with the job of plant reproduction.

Plants and flowers are clear evidence of the wonderful creativity and imagination of our God.

Responding

Plant life can be helpful in reminding us to look again at how we are living our lives and also not to worry.

The prophet Hosea, when trying to help God's people see how they should live, used the image of planting: "Sow for yourselves righteousness; reap steadfast love; break up your fallow ground; for it is time to seek the LORD, that he may come and rain righteousness upon you" (Hosea 10:12).

A helpful spiritual question for me may be: What am *I* "planting" and what am *I* "reaping" in my life? When I look at how I spend my time and my money and what is really important in my life, how does that match with what I *say* is important to me? I take a look, for example, at how I treat others in my life, especially those who have been irritating me lately or those who may be in need. The book of Sirach reminds us, ". . . kindness is like a garden of blessings, and almsgiving endures forever" (40:17).

And Jesus, when talking about the way God takes care of us, pointed out some wild flowers as examples:

> He said to his disciples, "Therefore I tell you, do not worry about your life, what you will eat, or about your body, what you will wear. For life is more than food, and the body more than clothing. . . . And can any of you by worrying add a single hour to your span of life? If then you are not able to do so small a thing as that, why do you worry about the rest? Consider the lilies, how they grow: they neither toil nor spin; yet I tell you, even Solomon in all his glory was not clothed like one of these. But if God so clothes the grass of the field, which is alive today and tomorrow is thrown into the oven, how much more will he clothe you—you of little faith!" (Luke 12:22-23, 25-28)

What is it that I've been worrying about lately that I can't really do anything about and need to let go of and give to God?

Nurturing God of all life, thank you for the wonderful variety of plants that you have given us to use and enjoy. Bless all those who work with plants and flowers, whether for delight and beauty or for food.

Please help me to "root" my life in your love and show respect and care to all I meet, even to those who may seem like "weeds" in my life at times. And help me not to worry about my life because I know that you are always taking care of me more than I can even imagine. Amen.

Soil or Dirt: Grounded in Love

Materials at hand: A small amount of dirt from outside or some potting soil, with a candle as a prayer focus.

Centering

(Light the candle and with your hands spread open say:)
Loving God, Creator of all that is,
here I am—today, in this place,
with all the senses you have given me.
Help me to use them to come to experience you more deeply.
You are present everywhere around me;
open me to know more of the many ways
that your goodness surrounds me.
Thank you for this time to be with you and to listen to you.
Amen.

Savoring

Look at the soil as it sits before you. Notice its texture and any variation in it or its color. Is it sandy? Coarse? Rocky? Does it have any clay in it? Any peat moss or wood chips? Is it wet or dry?

Smell it. Can you smell the rich smell of "fertile" possibilities for growth, and is the smell what you would have expected?

Next take time to touch it, first lightly on the top of it; try to concentrate on the information you are getting through your fingertips. Then sift the soil through your fingers. What do you feel, and is it much different from the way you expected it to feel?

Try to imagine the complex process that has led to the existence of this rich substance; think of all the life that helped contribute to its formation and all the life that it will help support in the future.

Listening

Listen to and reflect on one or more of these passages as you watch the candlelight play across the pile of soil:

Then the LORD God formed man from the dust of the ground, and breathed into his nostrils the breath of life; and the man became a living being. (Genesis 2:7)

*

Do not fear, O soil; be glad and rejoice, for the LORD has done great things! Do not fear, you animals of the field, for the pastures of the wilderness are green; the tree bears its fruit, the fig tree and vine give their full yield. (Joel 2:21-22)

*

"A sower went out to sow his seed; and as he sowed, some fell on the path and was trampled on, and the birds of the air ate it up. Some fell on the rock; and as it grew up, it withered for lack of moisture. Some fell among thorns, and the thorns grew with it and choked it. Some fell into good soil, and when it grew, it produced a hundredfold." As he said this, he called out, "Let anyone with ears to hear listen!" . . .

"Now the parable is this: The seed is the word of God. The ones on the path are those who have heard; then the devil comes and takes away the word from their hearts, so that they may not believe and be saved. The ones on the rock are those who, when they hear the word, receive it with joy. But these have no root; they believe only for a while and in a time of testing fall away. As for what fell among the thorns, these are the ones who hear; but as they go on their way, they are choked by the cares and riches and pleasures of life, and their fruit does not mature. But as for that in the good soil, these are the ones who, when they hear the word, hold it fast in an honest and good heart, and bear fruit with patient endurance." (Luke 8:5-8, 11-15)

*

As he walked along, he saw a man blind from birth. His disciples asked him, "Rabbi, who sinned, this man or his parents, that he was born blind?" Jesus answered, "Neither this man nor his parents sinned; he was born blind so that God's works might be revealed in him. We must work the works of him who sent me while it is day; night is coming when no one can work. As long as I am in the world, I am the light of the world." When he had said this, he spat on the ground and made mud with the saliva and spread the mud on the man's eyes, saying to him, "Go, wash in the pool of Siloam" (which means Sent). Then [the man] went and washed and came back able to see. (John 9:1-7)

Considering

This soil which lies before you and also covers the earth is largely the product of disintegration, both of rocks that have been broken down by the process of freezing and thawing and also of decaying organic matter which has had the help of bacteria and fungi to make it ready for supporting more life. It is a veritable chemical laboratory, with a large number of reactions happening within it, and it produces several gases such as oxygen, nitrogen, and carbon dioxide.

Soils can vary widely in their appearance, their fertility, their chemical characteristics, such as their mineral and organic content, and even the amount of water that they can hold. Conditions such as over-cultivation or fires can deprive the soil of its natural protection from erosion and can endanger all the ecosystems that depend on the soil.

Loving God of the wind and the rain, help us to appreciate the delicate and precious gift that our soil is.

Responding

The creation account in the second chapter of Genesis shows God breathing the Spirit into dust from the ground (*adamah* in Hebrew) and creating a human (*adam* in Hebrew); this account reminds us that in a sense we are mud that breathes and that we are indeed very close to the earth. This has important implications for our spirituality.

For example, being close to the earth, such as at a park or out in nature or even working in the garden, can be for many people an especially helpful place for prayer and for feeling connected with their spirituality.

The word "humility" comes from the word "humus," or soil. An attitude of humility is one that waits patiently for God as the soil waits for sun and rain. Humility doesn't mean putting oneself down or merely being passive; it just means that I know what I'm in charge of and also what God is.

As I consider the following passage, help me to examine my own need for an authentic humility, one that sees everything in my life as gift but doesn't deny or downplay the gifts that I have:

> As God's chosen ones, holy and beloved, clothe your-selves with compassion, kindness, humility, meekness, and patience. Bear with one another and, if anyone has a complaint against another, forgive each other; just as the Lord has forgiven you, so you also must forgive. Above all, clothe yourselves with love, which binds everything together in perfect harmony. (Colossians 3:12-14)

Are there some ways that I can be a better steward of the earth in my own yard (if you have one) or in my community by helping with recycling or composting or projects to help clean up what we humans have done to our environment? I remember all those who work with the soil in my prayers and thoughts, both those who farm—often under difficult circumstances—and those who work for a better and cleaner environment for all of us.

Loving God of all that grows, thank you for the rich gift of the soil that helps support all life on this planet. Amen.

Sunshine: Energy From God

Materials at hand: On a sunny day, sit outside in the sun or sit inside by a window (if it's not sunny, use a picture or drawing of the sun), with a candle as a prayer focus.

Centering

(Light the candle and with your hands spread open say:)
Loving God, Creator of all that is,
here I am—today, in this place,
with all the senses you have given me.
Help me to use them to come to experience you more deeply.
You are present everywhere around me;
open me to know more of the many ways
that your goodness surrounds me.
Thank you for this time to be with you and to listen to you.
Amen.

Savoring

Spend some time just basking in the sun's rays, if it's out, and if it's not a sunny day, try to remember what that feels like to just sit and soak up the sun's energy. Feel it warm you through and through, which may take some imagination on a colder day. Think about how much of a gift our sun is to each of us and to the earth, a gift we usually think about only when it is suddenly obscured by a cloud or hidden on an overcast day.

Visualize and try to feel what it would be like to be a cold piece of ground that welcomes the sun in the morning and is gradually warmed by its presence through the day, a piece of ground complete with plants and flowers that stretch toward the energy pouring from this source of light and warmth.

Listening

Listen to and reflect on one or more of these passages as you watch the candlelight or the sunlight play across the space before you:

> The heavens are telling the glory of God; and the firmament proclaims his handiwork. Day to day pours forth speech, and night to night declares knowledge. There is no speech, nor are there words; their voice is not heard; yet their voice goes out through all the earth, and their words to the end of the world. In the heavens he has set a tent for the sun, which comes out like a bridegroom from his wedding canopy, and like a strong man runs its course with joy. Its rising is from the end of the heavens, and its circuit to the end of them; and nothing is hid from its heat. (Psalm 19:1-6)
>
> *
>
> Praise the LORD! Praise, O servants of the LORD; praise the name of the LORD. Blessed be the name of the LORD from this time on and forevermore. From the rising of the sun to its setting the name of the LORD is to be praised. (Psalm 113:1-3)
>
> *
>
> The sun, when it appears, proclaims as it rises what a marvelous instrument it is, the work of the Most High. At noon it parches the land, and who can withstand its burning heat? A man tending a furnace works in burning heat, but three times as hot is the sun scorching the mountains; it breathes out fiery vapors, and its bright rays blind the eyes. Great is the Lord who made it; at his orders it hurries on its course. (Sirach 43:2-5)
>
> *
>
> Praise him, sun and moon; praise him, all you shining stars! (Psalm 148:3)

Considering

The sun is our closest star, one of hundreds of millions in our Milky Way galaxy alone, which is, in turn, one of about that many other similar galaxies in our universe. When we think about the fact that if the sun were any closer we would bake and if it were any farther away from us we would freeze, the wonder of our relationship with this star becomes even more amazing.

We have learned far more about the sun than we knew when Galileo first observed sunspots through the newly invented telescope in 1611, although Chinese astronomers had already described them before the birth of Christ. We know, for example, that it is composed primarily of hydrogen and helium gases and has enough energy to last another 4.5 billion years before it begins to change and burn out.

Ancient cultures worshiped the sun, and we know that it has been important to human culture and to our sense of time and growth since ancient times. It is directly or indirectly responsible for all the sources of energy on earth, and without it our world would simply die.

Responding

The book of Ecclesiastes (1:9) pessimistically tells us that there is nothing new under the sun, but a couple other passages from scripture remind us of the need to care for our enemies and to tell the truth when we look at our relationships "in light of" the sun.

Matthew's gospel points out, "But I say to you, Love your enemies and pray for those who persecute you, so that you may be children of your Father in heaven; for he makes his sun rise on the evil and on the good, and sends rain on the righteous and on the unrighteous" (Matthew 5:44-45).

And in St. Paul's letter to the Ephesians, he encourages them in their relationships with one another, "So then, putting away falsehood, let all of us speak the truth to our neighbors, for we are members of one another. Be angry but do not sin; do not let the sun go down on your anger, and do not make room for the devil" (Ephesians 4:25-27).

How am I called to love my enemies, those who irritate and test my patience, and how am I called to tell the truth and not dwell in anger? "Enlighten" me, loving God, so that I can look a bit more with your eyes at my relationships and how I should be treating others. Help me understand at least one specific way that I can change the way I relate to someone in my life.

God of all the planets and the universe, bless those peoples in the parts of the world closest to the sun near the equator, and also bless the scientists who study the sun, solar energy, and those exploring what can be done to halt the depletion of the ozone layer which helps protect the earth from the sun's cancer-causing ultraviolet rays. Help me to "bask" in the warmth of your love whenever I see the sun. Amen.

Rain: On the Just and Unjust

Materials at hand: On a rainy day, sit by a window (if it's not raining, use an umbrella or a rain hat as a reminder), with a candle as a prayer focus.

Centering
(Light the candle and with your hands spread open say:)
Loving God, Creator of all that is,
here I am—today, in this place,
with all the senses you have given me.
Help me to use them to come to experience you more deeply.
You are present everywhere around me;
open me to know more of the many ways
that your goodness surrounds me.
Thank you for this time to be with you and to listen to you.
Amen.

Savoring
If it's raining, make things as quiet as possible and listen to the rain. If it's possible, step outside and listen to how it sounds as it hits various kinds of surfaces: leaves, rocks, cement, dirt, and even the roof—or gutters or downspouts, if you have them.

What does the rain smell like? Does it always smell this way? Is it different in a thunderstorm?

Feel the rain—at least with your hand, if not your face. How would you characterize this rain between a light mist and a drenching downpour? (If you're really feeling adventurous and it's a light rain, lie down and experience the rain drifting slowly down to you, the way the earth receives and experiences the rain!)

As you watch the rain, try to imagine all the water this must involve. Have you ever tried to count just the drops you can see, not to mention all those you can't see? Think of the journey each drop must travel from far up in the sky down to the ground, washing impurities out of the air as it comes and then washing dirt and dust from whatever it lands upon.

If it isn't raining, try to imagine the umbrella or rain hat soaking wet and then think about everything outside being wet, the skies turning dark, the streets running with water, and all the plants and flowers and grass getting a soaking as well as a good, long drink. Try to remember the sounds and smells of a rainy day.

Listening

Listen to and reflect on one or more of these passages as you watch the candle and the rain (or imagine it):

> Sing to the LORD with thanksgiving; make melody to our God on the lyre. He covers the heavens with clouds, prepares rain for the earth, makes grass grow on the hills. (Psalm 147:7-8)
>
> *
>
> Shower, O heavens, from above, and let the skies rain down righteousness; let the earth open, that salvation may spring up, and let it cause righteousness to sprout up also; I the LORD have created it. . . . For as the rain and the snow come down from heaven, and do not return there until they have watered the earth, making it bring forth and sprout, giving seed to the sower and bread to the eater, so shall my word be that goes out from my mouth; it shall not return to me empty, but it shall accomplish that which I purpose, and succeed in the thing for which I sent it. (Isaiah 45:8; 55:10-11)
>
> *
>
> Surely God is great. . . . For he draws up the drops of water; he distills his mist in rain, which the skies pour down and drop upon mortals abundantly. Can anyone understand the spreading of the clouds, the thunderings of his pavilion? For by these . . . he gives food in abundance. (Job 36:26-29, 31)
>
> *
>
> "Bless the Lord, all rain and dew; sing praise to him and highly exalt him forever." (Daniel 3:64)

Considering

Rain is a wonderful and necessary gift to us. Even though it may spoil or at least postpone our outdoor plans on occasion, without it all life on our earth would eventually cease, and it doesn't take too long without rain before a serious drought can develop. Rainfall is one of the main factors in determining climates throughout our world, and it can vary considerably from one year to the next.

The water cycle that involves storage on and in the earth, evaporation as water vapor into the atmosphere, condensation and precipitation as rain, snow, or hail, and then runoff into rivers and other places where water is stored is both complex and yet essential to our lives. Even with technological advances in irrigation and crop management to help cope with less rain, a change in rain patterns affects us all.

Since rain is something that we can neither earn nor control, it is a helpful image of God's gift of love and grace, love that is not earned or controlled in any way by us.

Responding

If God's love for us is as free and as generous as the rain, that has strong implications for the way we are called to love others in turn. Jesus reminds us:

> "You have heard that it was said, 'You shall love your neighbor and hate your enemy.' But I say to you, Love your enemies and pray for those who persecute you, so that you may be children of your Father in heaven; for he makes his sun rise on the evil and on the good, and sends rain on the righteous and on the unrighteous. For if you love those who love you, what reward do you have? Do not even the tax collectors do the same? And if you greet only your brothers and sisters, what more are you doing than others? Do not even the Gentiles do the same?" (Matthew 5:43-47)

How can I take these words to heart and work on stretching my categories of who is worthy of my care and love beyond those I usually think of? This week I will pray for and show special care to one or two people who are really irritating for me.

God of the drizzle and the downpour, "shower" your love and understanding down upon me, and please help me to remember the extravagance and generosity of your love for me and for everyone, especially whenever it rains. Bless all those who cope with too little or too much rain at this time and all those who work with the environment and issues such as acid rain. Amen.

Rock: A Solid Foundation

Materials at hand: A rock of any size, with a candle as a prayer focus.

Centering

(Light the candle and with your hands spread open say:)
Loving God, Creator of all that is,
here I am—today, in this place,
with all the senses you have given me.
Help me to use them to come to experience you more deeply.
You are present everywhere around me;
open me to know more of the many ways
that your goodness surrounds me.
Thank you for this time to be with you and to listen to you.
Amen.

Savoring

Take a look at the rock sitting before you as though you had never seen it before. Note its shape and color and texture. What would you guess about its weight just by its appearance? Now explore it with your fingertips with your eyes closed. Pick it up and hold it while your eyes are still shut. How does the rock feel in your hand? Do you have enough information through touch now to be able to pick this rock out from among a group of other rocks?

As you open your eyes, see what other information you can gain about this piece of stone. What color differences are there? Are there any veins of other minerals or spots on the rock or distinctive markings that you would have missed without the sense of sight?

What do you think this rock has "seen" and what stories could it tell if it could speak?

What could be more common than a rock—or is it?

Listening

Listen to and reflect on one or more of these passages as you watch the candlelight play across the rock:

> The LORD is my rock, my fortress, and my deliverer, my God, my rock in whom I take refuge, my shield, and the horn of my salvation, my stronghold. (Psalm 18:2)
>
> *
>
> Thus says the Lord GOD: I will gather you from the peoples, and assemble you out of the countries where you have been scattered, and I will give you the land of Israel. . . . I will give them one heart, and put a new spirit within them; I will remove the heart of stone from their flesh and give them a heart of flesh, so that they may follow my statutes and keep my ordinances and obey them. Then they shall be my people, and I will be their God. (Ezekiel 11:17, 19-20)
>
> *
>
> "I will show you what someone is like who comes to me, hears my words, and acts on them. That one is like a man building a house, who dug deeply and laid the foundation on rock; when a flood arose, the river burst against that house but could not shake it, because it had been well built." (Luke 6:47-48)
>
> *
>
> Come to [Jesus], a living stone, though rejected by mortals yet chosen and precious in God's sight, and like living stones, let yourselves be built into a spiritual house . . . . For it stands in scripture: "See, I am laying in Zion a stone, a cornerstone chosen and precious; and whoever believes in him will not be put to shame." To you then who believe, he is precious; but for those who do not believe, "The stone that the builders rejected has become the very head of the corner," and "A stone that makes them stumble, and a rock that makes them fall." (1 Peter 2:4-8)

Considering

Rocks come in endless shapes and sizes throughout the world. There are three main kinds of rock, based on different origins.

SAVORING GOD

Sedimentary rock comes from the gradual accumulation of minerals and particles over the centuries, and often the layers of sediment can be seen in the rock. Igneous rocks were once molten material called magma, which cooled and solidified, and the speed with which it did so can make a difference in its consistency. Metamorphic rock is a result of one of the other two kinds of rock then being under extreme conditions of heat and pressure; marble is an example of metamorphic rock.

Whether one collects rocks or just notices them occasionally, from tiny grains of sand to huge boulders, rocks are interesting objects, and they provide the foundation for our earth. There's something comforting about rock; it's "rock solid," as we say. Many of our most important buildings—religious and secular—are built of stone, to give a strong, lasting feel to the building as it surrounds us.

In the rough terrain of the Holy Land, having a position on a rocky crag when fighting meant having the edge over one's enemies, and calling God a Rock in scripture meant that God was the source of safety and security in times of trouble.

Responding

Rocks can help serve as reminders both about the importance of prayer and of not judging others.

When it comes to prayer, sometimes it's easy to give up or wonder whether it's worth our energy. In Matthew's gospel Jesus reminds us that we can always ask God for what we need:

> "Ask, and it will be given you; search, and you will find; knock, and the door will be opened for you. For everyone who asks receives, and everyone who searches finds, and for everyone who knocks, the door will be opened. Is there anyone among you who, if your child asks for bread, will give a stone? Or if the child asks for a fish, will give a snake? If you then, who are evil, know how to give good gifts to your children, how much more will your Father in heaven give good things to those who ask him!"
> (Matthew 7:7-11)

48

What is there that I would like to ask God but have been afraid or reluctant to do so?

Confidence in prayer and deep trust in God is a long-term process, as the prophet Ezekiel reminded us. We know that real conversion of our hearts is not just a once-and-for-all experience, but one that happens over and over in our lives, when we change our hearts of stone—the ways that we can too easily take God and God's blessings for granted—for hearts of flesh—ones that realize once again all the gifts our God gives us and wants us to have.

In John's gospel, a stone also becomes a reminder not to judge others but rather to leave that for God, since none of us is perfect. A woman caught in the act of the sin of adultery was brought to Jesus, but the focus in the gospel shifts from her to those who brought her and were eager to condemn her and to have Jesus do so. We hear how he responds to their question about what should be done with her:

> Jesus bent down and wrote with his finger on the ground. When they kept on questioning him, he straightened up and said to them, "Let anyone among you who is without sin be the first to throw a stone at her." And once again he bent down and wrote on the ground. When they heard it, they went away, one by one, beginning with the elders; and Jesus was left alone with the woman standing before him. Jesus straightened up and said to her, "Woman, where are they? Has no one condemned you?" She said, "No one, sir." And Jesus said, "Neither do I condemn you. Go your way, and from now on do not sin again." (John 8:6-11)

Loving and generous God, you invite me to change my heart, to ask for what I need and not to worry about others' faults but to be aware of my own. Help this stone to remind me of all that you are calling me to. Bless all those who work with rock and stone, those working in mines and those who climb rocks and mountains. Please help me have a faith that is "rock solid." Amen.

Clouds: Sign of God's Presence

Materials at hand: Sit by the window if there are clouds visible or use a picture of clouds, with a candle as a prayer focus.

Centering

(Light the candle and with your hands spread open say:)
Loving God, Creator of all that is,
here I am—today, in this place,
with all the senses you have given me.
Help me to use them to come to experience you more deeply.
You are present everywhere around me;
open me to know more of the many ways
that your goodness surrounds me.
Thank you for this time to be with you and to listen to you.
Amen.

Savoring

If there are clouds in the sky and the weather is fairly pleasant, go outside to watch them. Are they moving very fast or are they relatively stable? (When clouds seem to be moving fast from the ground, we know that they are going very fast indeed.) Are some of the clouds darker than others, and if it's sunset or sunrise, are there other colors besides white or gray? Are they fluffy or wispy, high or rather low? Are they solid across the sky or are there gaps between them where the sky shows through?

Can you see any particular shapes in the clouds? Do you have a favorite kind of cloud? If so, what kind is it? Have you ever seen a rainbow in the midst of the clouds?

If it's raining or too cold, watch the clouds from inside. (If you're using a picture of clouds, you really need to use your imagination.) Does a cloudy day have an effect on your moods? If so, what kind of effect? Have you had the experience of flying through, or beside, a cloud in a plane? How was that different, if at all, from what you expected?

Although having every day be sunny may sound ideal, we know that we need the clouds and the precipitation they bring to have the water we need for things to grow. Clouds are both fascinating and necessary.

Listening

Listen to and reflect on one or more of these passages as you watch the candlelight on a cloudy day or as it plays across the picture of the clouds:

> So God led the people [of Israel] by the roundabout way of the wilderness toward the Red Sea. . . . The LORD went in front of them in a pillar of cloud by day, to lead them along the way, and in a pillar of fire by night, to give them light, so that they might travel by day and by night. Neither the pillar of cloud by day nor the pillar of fire by night left its place in front of the people. (Exodus 13:18, 21-22)
>
> *
>
> And [Jesus] was transfigured before them, and his face shone like the sun, and his clothes became dazzling white. Suddenly there appeared to them Moses and Elijah, talking with him. Then Peter said to Jesus, "Lord, it is good for us to be here; if you wish, I will make three dwellings here, one for you, one for Moses, and one for Elijah." While he was still speaking, suddenly a bright cloud overshadowed them, and from the cloud a voice said, "This is my Son, the Beloved; with him I am well pleased; listen to him!" (Matthew 17:2-5)
>
> *
>
> "Bless the Lord, lightnings and clouds; sing praise to him and highly exalt him forever." (Daniel 3:73)
>
> *
>
> So when they had come together, [the disciples] asked [Jesus], "Lord, is this the time when you will restore the kingdom to Israel?" He replied, "It is not for you to know the times or periods

that the Father has set by his own authority. But you will receive power when the Holy Spirit has come upon you; and you will be my witnesses in Jerusalem, in all Judea and Samaria, and to the ends of the earth." When he had said this, as they were watching, he was lifted up, and a cloud took him out of their sight. (Acts 1:6-9)

*

Your steadfast love, O LORD, extends to the heavens, your faithfulness to the clouds. (Psalm 36:5)

*

Then God said to Noah and to his sons with him, "As for me, I am establishing my covenant with you and your descendants after you, and with every living creature that is with you, the birds, the domestic animals, and every animal of the earth with you, as many as came out of the ark. I establish my covenant with you, that never again shall all flesh be cut off by the waters of a flood, and never again shall there be a flood to destroy the earth." God said, "This is the sign of the covenant that I make between me and you and every living creature that is with you, for all future generations: I have set my bow in the clouds, and it shall be a sign of the covenant between me and the earth." (Genesis 9:8-13)

Considering

Clouds are moisture in the form of water droplets or ice crystals that are suspended in the air, and they are an important part of the water cycle which helps sustain the earth. The first attempts to classify clouds were in the nineteenth century, and there are over a hundred different kinds of clouds now recognized, based on such variables as their height, shape, and whether they contain water or ice crystals.

In the Jewish religious tradition God was often revealed in a cloud, such as the one that spoke to Moses on the mountain, giving him the Ten Commandments, and the one that led them through the desert, hovering over the tabernacle in the tent of the covenant. Perhaps the Jews, who were very un-abstract thinkers, saw a cloud as a way to help them imagine God's presence and care in a way that was visible while not tangible.

Clouds are helpful to the earth because they actually help protect the planet from absorbing too much of the sun's radiation. But there is more solar energy than one might think on a cloudy day, because much of the radiation that does make it through to the earth's surface

Clouds: Sign of God's Presence

is bounced back to the clouds, and they in turn reflect it back once again to the earth. As a result, there is actually more solar radiated heat energy absorbed on a cloudy day than on a sunny one. A gray, cloudy day helps us more than we may know.

Responding

Clouds are amazing to watch, especially on a sunny day as they head past the sun or hit some high-altitude winds and may begin to evaporate in the process. The prophet Isaiah tells us that is just how our faults and sins are before God's all-encompassing love, which is always more powerful than our mistakes:

> Remember these things, O Jacob, and Israel, for you are my servant; I formed you, you are my servant; O Israel, you will not be forgotten by me. I have swept away your transgressions like a cloud, and your sins like mist; return to me, for I have redeemed you. (Isaiah 44:21-22)

Tender and forgiving God, help me to better appreciate your love for me, which calls me to be more fully who I can be and which always forgives me. Help me to forgive myself as freely as you forgive me, especially when it comes to (name one specific area here that you need to work on forgiving yourself for).

God of all the skies, please bless those who study and work with clouds, from pilots to farmers. Bless all those who need the clouds for rain and also those who may feel "under the cloud" of depression; help them to get the help they need to cope with it.

Whenever I see clouds, help me to think of your presence, which is with me wherever I go. Amen.

Seeds: Life Within

Materials at hand: Seeds from the kitchen—such as dry beans, sesame or sunflower seeds—or any kind of nuts, or seeds gathered from outside, or seeds in a packet ready for planting; a candle as a prayer focus.

Centering

(Light the candle and with your hands spread open say:)
Loving God, Creator of all that is,
here I am—today, in this place,
with all the senses you have given me.
Help me to use them to come to experience you more deeply.
You are present everywhere around me;
open me to know more of the many ways
that your goodness surrounds me.
Thank you for this time to be with you and to listen to you.
Amen.

Savoring

Look at the seeds before you, at the possibility and promise packed into so small a "package." They wait with great patience for the chance to do what they were created to do: to be the source of new life and growth that seems impossible, given their size. If you didn't know what they were, they could easily be confused with a small pebble or some dust or dirt.

Pick up a couple seeds (or the package) and hold them in the palm of your hand; they are so small and helpless and yet they contain so much life. Feel how hard the shell is with your other hand, and yet this shell is able to soften and yield when needed to make way for growth.

Try to imagine what would happen if your hand were soil and there were sufficient water and warmth to begin the process of germination, the swelling and bursting forth of the new life that now lies bundled tight inside the seeds before you. Picture the water reaching the seed through rain that has fallen and the sun beginning to warm the soil that holds the seeds so gently. Imagine the slow but powerful process of the unfolding of life from within the seed that forces its way with a gradual but relentless power outward from its center, a power that can even break through pavement at times in order to reach air and light.

Feel the potential for power that God has given these seemingly lifeless and hard particles. You hold nothing less than miracles in your hand.

Listening

Listen to and reflect on one or more of these passages as you watch the candlelight play across the seeds:

> Then God said, "Let the earth put forth vegetation: plants yielding seed, and fruit trees of every kind on earth that bear fruit with the seed in it." And it was so. The earth brought forth vegetation: plants yielding seed of every kind, and trees of every kind bearing fruit with the seed in it. And God saw that it was good. . . . God said, "See, I have given you every plant yielding seed that is upon the face of all the earth, and every tree with seed in its fruit; you shall have them for food." (Genesis 1:11-12, 29)
>
> *
>
> For as the rain and the snow come down from heaven, and do not return there until they have watered the earth, making it bring forth and sprout, giving seed to the sower and bread to the eater, so shall my word be that goes out from my mouth; it shall not return to me empty, but it shall accomplish that which I purpose, and succeed in the thing for which I sent it. (Isaiah 55:10-11)
>
> *
>
> He put before them another parable: "The kingdom of heaven is like a mustard seed that someone took and sowed in his field; it is the smallest of all the seeds, but when it has grown it is the greatest

of shrubs and becomes a tree, so that the birds of the air come and make nests in its branches." (Matthew 13:31-32)

*

He also said, "The kingdom of God is as if someone would scatter seed on the ground, and would sleep and rise night and day, and the seed would sprout and grow, he does not know how. The earth produces of itself, first the stalk, then the head, then the full grain in the head. But when the grain is ripe, at once he goes in with his sickle, because the harvest has come." (Mark 4:26-29)

Considering

Each seed is a complete "package": it has all the information and energy it needs to make just the right kind of plant and nothing else. It is shelter (the seed coat), food source, and starter plant (the embryo) for the new possibility that lies within it. Once dispersed by the parent plant, the seeds may end up traveling in an amazing variety of ways—by air, water, or often "hitching a ride" with animal or human "hosts."

But in order for any seed to do what it was created to do, an important step must happen: it must die. In order to germinate it must be willing to be transformed, to cease to exist in the way that it had.

And it's true for us in our lives, too, as Jesus reminds us in John's gospel: "Very truly, I tell you, unless a grain of wheat falls into the earth and dies, it remains just a single grain; but if it dies, it bears much fruit. Those who love their life lose it, and those who hate their life in this world will keep it for eternal life" (John 12:24-25).

Whether it's the baby becoming the toddler, the toddler becoming the child and then the adolescent and young adult, or perhaps the hopes and dreams and expectations of a situation giving way to the actual experience, each new reality in our lives means a leaving behind, a shedding of the old reality before the new can be born. Dying to the old realities in our lives and rising to new possibilities sounds fine and even reasonable until we're faced with the actual reality. With Jesus in the garden at Gethsemane, we want to ask God to let this cup pass us by.

Responding

What are some ways in which this dying and rising so essential to the life of a seed and to my own life have taken place in the last six months or year? How am I doing in the process of dying to the old reality and rising to new life?

What about others I know and care about? Have there been some actual deaths or some losses and changes that are hard for them to adjust to, such as divorce or relocation or disappointments? Are there some ways that I can pray for these situations and perhaps show these people I care for them by a card or a call or a visit?

Loving God of all life, bless all those who work with seeds, producing them or sowing and harvesting. Bless, too, those having a hard time with the dying needed in order for new growth to happen. Help me to see you more clearly in the loss and dying in my life as well as the new possibilities that arise, and in the midst of this dying and rising help me to know your comforting presence constantly inviting me to grow. Amen.

Snow: White Wonder

Materials at hand: On a snowy day, sit near the window or bring some snow inside (if it's not snowing—or it doesn't where you live— use a picture of a snowy scene or of a snowman, or even a paper snowflake), with a candle as a prayer focus.

Centering

(Light the candle and with your hands spread open say:)
Loving God, Creator of all that is,
here I am—today, in this place,
with all the senses you have given me.
Help me to use them to come to experience you more deeply.
You are present everywhere around me;
open me to know more of the many ways
that your goodness surrounds me.
Thank you for this time to be with you and to listen to you.
Amen.

Savoring

If it's snowing, sit quietly and watch it come down—or go out and watch it transform the landscape. Catch some snow on your hand or on your tongue. Depending on the temperature outside, the snow may actually make it seem warmer than it would be otherwise.

Listen carefully to see if the snow makes a sound as it falls; sometimes it does. It also changes the sounds outside; listen to how they are muffled and softer, and yet you can hear sounds from farther away, especially with newly fallen snow.

Watch what the whiteness does to the light outside and to colors, which can easily become more stark, more black and white—or dark and white—than before. Look especially at the bare branches on the trees and any plants or weeds that you can see; notice how graceful and lacy these become against the snow.

If it's not snowing, try to imagine how it feels in the snow with the white coldness all around you falling everywhere. Remember the feeling of bundling up before—and unbundling after—going out into the transformed world. Remember shoveling and sledding and slipping around. Snow can transform our world and the way we look at it in a surprisingly short amount of time.

Listening

Listen to and reflect on one or more of these passages as you watch the candlelight and the snow (or imagine it):

> [God] sends out his command to the earth; his word runs swiftly. He gives snow like wool; he scatters frost like ashes. He hurls down hail like crumbs—who can stand before his cold? He sends out his word, and melts them; he makes his wind blow, and the waters flow. (Psalm 147:15-18)
>
> *
>
> By [God's] command he sends the driving snow and speeds the lightnings of his judgment. . . . He scatters the snow like birds flying down, and its descent is like locusts alighting. The eye is dazzled by the beauty of its whiteness, and the mind is amazed as it falls. He pours frost over the earth like salt, and icicles form like pointed thorns. The cold north wind blows, and ice freezes on the water; it settles on every pool of water, and the water puts it on like a breastplate. (Sirach 43:13, 17-20)
>
> *
>
> "Bless the Lord, ice and cold; sing praise to him and highly exalt him forever. Bless the Lord, frosts and snows; sing praise to him and highly exalt him forever." (Daniel 3:69-70)

Considering

Snow is actually ice crystals that have gathered themselves around a bit of dust when the air temperature is below the freezing level for water. Although snow usually looks white, it is actually transparent.

It is the reflection of light off the many sides of its hexagonal crystals that makes it appear white.

While all snowflakes are symmetrical and all have six sides, each one is unique in its appearance, due in part to varying weather conditions and the way the ice crystals build on top of one another. There is so much air trapped within and between snowflakes that it usually takes ten to twelve inches of snow to result in one inch of water when melted.

Snow is a rarity in the biblical lands of the Middle East, except in the mountains. Wherever it does fall, snow is an important source of water as it melts in the mountains and flows downhill in streams. It also serves as a good insulator, protecting plants and hibernating animals from the cold winter air.

Although it may be a mess to drive in, snow is both beautiful and fun, a world of wonder in which we can walk and ski and sled.

Responding

The clean and bright image of snow is used in Psalm 51 to describe the way we feel when we realize that God forgives our faults and sins, which was often symbolized by being sprinkled with hyssop, an ancient herb:

> Hide your face from my sins, and blot out all my iniquities. Create in me a clean heart, O God, and put a new and right spirit within me. Do not cast me away from your presence, and do not take your holy spirit from me. Restore to me the joy of your salvation, and sustain in me a willing spirit. . . . Purge me with hyssop, and I shall be clean; wash me, and I shall be whiter than snow. (Psalm 51:9-12, 7)

Each of us is only too aware of our faults and failings; we come face to face with them every day, although we'd rather not. But God's love is not limited by how selfish or fearful, lazy or unlovable we may act or feel. God's love is bigger than anything I can do to hide from it.

Snow: White Wonder

Just as the snow covers everything as it is and makes it white and beautiful, God's love takes me where I am and loves the beautiful me buried deep inside of what can seem like a real mess some days.

God of snow and ice, thank you for your wonderful gift of snow. Please bless those peoples of the north and the mountains who live with a great deal of snow and those who suffer from the cold weather, wherever they are. And bless those working to help end global warming, especially as it now affects our North and South Poles. Bless all skiers and skaters and anyone else who especially enjoys snow and ice.

God of winter and cold, please help me to remember the warmth of your faithful, forgiving love for me when I see the bright, white snow. Amen.

Wind or Fan:
The Power of the Spirit

Materials at hand: Sit by the window or go outside on a windy day (or use a fan to feel the air move), with a candle as a prayer focus.

Centering

(Light the candle and with your hands spread open say:)
Loving God, Creator of all that is,
here I am—today, in this place,
with all the senses you have given me.
Help me to use them to come to experience you more deeply.
You are present everywhere around me;
open me to know more of the many ways
that your goodness surrounds me.
Thank you for this time to be with you and to listen to you.
Amen.

Savoring

Whether the wind is blowing or you are using a fan, watch what happens when air is moving. Notice that anything that is loose or flexible will move, whether leaves or hair or branches or a piece of paper. We can't really *see* the wind; all we can see are the *effects* of the wind that let us know the air is moving, sometimes quite briskly.

Try to feel the wind or air on your face as though for the very first time. How would you describe this experience to someone who had never felt it? Would you say that the air caresses your face and body, or does it seem more forceful than that to you? Have you ever been in a wind so strong or so cold that it was hard to breathe? How did that feel?

Depending on its timing and severity and whether you've got a kite or a sailboat at the ready, wind can be either a frustration or a blessing.

Listening

Listen to and reflect on one or more of these passages as you watch the flame of the candle dance as the air moves:

In the beginning when God created the heavens and the earth, the earth was a formless void and darkness covered the face of the deep, while a wind from God swept over the face of the waters. (Genesis 1:1-2)

*

Bless the LORD, O my soul. O LORD my God, you are very great. You are clothed with honor and majesty, . . . you ride on the wings of the wind, you make the winds your messengers, fire and flame your ministers. (Psalm 104:1, 3-4)

*

On that day, when evening had come, [Jesus] said to [his disciples], "Let us go across to the other side." And leaving the crowd behind, they took him with them in the boat, just as he was. . . . A great windstorm arose, and the waves beat into the boat, so that the boat was already being swamped. But he was in the stern, asleep on the cushion; and they woke him up and said to him, "Teacher, do you not care that we are perishing?" He woke up and rebuked the wind, and said to the sea, "Peace! Be still!" Then the wind ceased, and there was a dead calm. He said to them, "Why are you afraid? Have you still no faith?" And they were filled with great awe and said to one another, "Who then is this, that even the wind and the sea obey him?" (Mark 4:35-41)

*

"Bless the Lord, all you winds; sing praise to him and highly exalt him forever." (Daniel 3:65)

*

Jesus answered [Nicodemus], "Very truly, I tell you, no one can enter the kingdom of God without being born of water and Spirit. What is born of the flesh is flesh, and what is born of the Spirit is spirit. Do not be astonished that I said to you, 'You must be born from above.' The wind blows where it chooses, and you hear the sound of it, but you do not know where it comes from or where it goes. So it is with everyone who is born of the Spirit." (John 3:5-8)

*

When the day of Pentecost had come, they were all together in one place. And suddenly from heaven there came a sound like the rush of a violent wind, and it filled the entire house where they were sitting. All of them were filled with the Holy Spirit and began to speak in other languages, as the Spirit gave them ability. (Acts 2:1-2, 4)

Considering

Wind is air in motion, caused by differences in atmospheric pressure, which is in turn mainly caused by temperature differences in the land or water below the air. There are many different kinds of winds, and the direction from which they blow varies generally according to where in the world they are located. The force and speed of the wind can vary considerably from a light breeze to a powerfully destructive cyclone, and its effects can make quite a difference in our lives.

On hot days any wind or movement of air is welcome because it can help relieve the feeling of heat. On the other hand, in cold weather, the wind chill factor is a way for scientists to include the wind in the colder temperatures because our bodies tend to lose heat faster when the wind is blowing.

In the ancient Hebrew language the word *Ruah* meant air in motion and was used to talk about the wind but also human breath. Gradually, it also referred to God's Spirit, which was mysterious and powerful, but the effects of the Spirit were all that were visible, like the wind. This Spirit was there at the creation in Genesis, hovering over the waters, and it was also bringing about a new creation and new energy in the community of believers gathered after Jesus' ascension.

Air in motion—whether it's the wind, our own breath, or God's Spirit—changes things.

Responding

Sometimes a strong wind can feel like it's pushing us around. The letter of James uses that image to encourage us to hold strong in our faith even when life can seem to be "pushing us around":

> My brothers and sisters, whenever you face trials of any kind, consider it nothing but joy, because you know that the testing of your faith produces endurance; and let endurance have its full effect, so that you may be mature and complete, lacking in nothing.
>
> If any of you is lacking in wisdom, ask God, who gives to all generously and ungrudgingly, and it will be given you. But ask in faith, never doubting, for the one who doubts is like a wave of the sea, driven and tossed by the wind. . . . (James 1:2-6)

God of wind and air and breath, thank you for the ability to breathe and be alive. Bless all those who have difficulty breathing because of asthma, emphysema, or other diseases, and bless all those who help them. Bless and protect those who live in places that experience strong and destructive winds such as hurricanes and tornadoes. Bless, too, all who travel on the wind, whether by hot air balloons, parachutes, wind surfing, or sailboats or those who fly in airplanes or helicopters; help them to be safe and healthy.

And when it comes to my faith and my relationships with others, dear God, keep me strong and constant in my commitments so that I am not pulled just "any way the wind blows." Amen.

Praying With
Personal Objects

Mirror: Who Am I?

Materials at hand: A mirror (preferably a hand mirror or a pocket one), with a candle as a prayer focus.

Centering

(Light the candle and with your hands spread open say:)
Loving God, Creator of all that is,
here I am—today, in this place,
with all the senses you have given me.
Help me to use them to come to experience you more deeply.
You are present everywhere around me;
open me to know more of the many ways
that your goodness surrounds me.
Thank you for this time to be with you and to listen to you.
Amen.

Savoring

Watch the candle's flame reflected in the mirror. Bounce the light from the flame around the room by moving the mirror. Notice how you can see any part of the room through the mirror—even the part behind you—by how you hold it. Are there new aspects of the space where you are that you may have never noticed before as you see them through the mirror?

See and feel the smoothness of the surface of the mirror. If there were any imperfections in the surface, it would not reflect without distortion. If possible, put the candle on the mirror and watch it reflect multiple candle flames. Think about other shiny surfaces that at times may function as mirrors, such as windows or glasses in bright sunlight or even the still surface of the water by moonlight.

Look at your own face in the mirror. Trace the outline of your face and features with your eyes or with your fingers on the glass. Are there any adjectives that come to mind as you look at your own face?

Listening

Listen to and reflect on one or more of these passages as you watch the candlelight play across the mirror:

> So God created humankind in his image, in the image of God he created them; male and female he created them. (Genesis 1:27)
>
> *
>
> For [wisdom] is a reflection of eternal light, a spotless mirror of the working of God, and an image of his goodness. (Wisdom 7:26)
>
> *
>
> "Why do you see the speck in your neighbor's eye, but do not notice the log in your own eye? Or how can you say to your neighbor, 'Friend, let me take out the speck in your eye,' when you yourself do not see the log in your own eye? You hypocrite, first take the log out of your own eye, and then you will see clearly to take the speck out of your neighbor's eye." (Luke 6:41-42)
>
> *
>
> Love never ends. But as for prophecies, they will come to an end; as for tongues, they will cease; as for knowledge, it will come to an end. For we know only in part, and we prophesy only in part; but when the complete comes, the partial will come to an end. . . . For now we see in a mirror, dimly, but then we will see face to face. Now I know only in part; then I will know fully, even as I have been fully known. (1 Corinthians 13:8-10, 12)

Considering

In ancient times mirrors were made of polished metal and usually possessed by only the wealthy. Today our mirrors are made of glass coated with metal, usually silver. Not only are they common in our homes, but our stores and malls also have a plentiful supply of them for us to check our appearance on a regular basis!

Mirrors can be quite useful; they allow us to expand our sight and to bend light in some important and constructive ways. We use mirrors in both telescopes and microscopes, as well as in lighthouses, headlights, and flashlights, for example.

However, it is also easy to become over-focused on your appearance in a society where mirrors are so plentiful. It can be tempting to fall into the trap that Narcissus did in Greek mythology, falling hopelessly in love with his own reflection in a pool.

How *do* we "see" ourselves accurately and realistically, so that we know both our gifts and our faults accurately and don't get preoccupied by either? With a clear sense of ourselves we can give more freely to others, not concerned about whether we're okay or not, but also not letting others take advantage of us, either. This clarity is the beginning of true wisdom.

Responding

In the letter of James, we read:

> . . . be doers of the word, and not merely hearers who deceive themselves. For if any are hearers of the word and not doers, they are like those who look at themselves in a mirror; for they look at themselves and, on going away, immediately forget what they were like. But those who look into the perfect law, the law of liberty, and persevere, being not hearers who forget but doers who act—they will be blessed in their doing. (James 1:22-25)

When I look in the mirror, O loving God, help me to see that you have made me in your image and that the way for me to truly reflect your love is to care for others with the same complete love that you have for me, no matter what my faults or imperfections.

Bless all those who make and sell mirrors. Help all those who use mirrors to properly see their own goodness. And help me to continue to grow in love so that I can more completely reflect you in all that I do. Amen.

Hand: God's Loving Generosity

Materials at hand: Your hand, with a candle as a prayer focus.

Centering

(Light the candle and with your hands spread open say:)
Loving God, Creator of all that is,
here I am—today, in this place,
with all the senses you have given me.
Help me to use them to come to experience you more deeply.
You are present everywhere around me;
open me to know more of the many ways
that your goodness surrounds me.
Thank you for this time to be with you and to listen to you.
Amen.

Savoring

Stretch out one of your hands and take a close look. Observe the veins and wrinkles, the scars (if any), the lines in your palm, your nail cuticles, and even your knuckles. Turn your hand over slowly and flex it, watching the amazing complexity of the range of motions and stretching of which your hand is capable.

Smell your hand; are there any signs of what you have been doing recently with your hands? Listen as you snap your fingers and clap your hands together, and think of all the kinds of information your hand helps with, from waving at a friend, motioning someone to come closer, telling someone to stop or that things are okay. You use your hand for an incredible variety of tasks in the course of a day.

Touch this hand with the other as though it were someone else's. What does touch reveal that your eye may have missed?

Your hand is indeed a wonderful "tool."

Listening

Listen to and reflect on one or more of these passages as you watch the candlelight play across your hand:

Into your hand I commit my spirit; you have redeemed me, O LORD, faithful God. (Psalm 31:5)

*

If I take the wings of the morning and settle at the farthest limits of the sea, even there your hand shall lead me, and your right hand shall hold me fast. (Psalm 139:9-10)

*

The eyes of all look to you, and you give them their food in due season. You open your hand, satisfying the desire of every living thing. (Psalm 145:15-16)

*

So the other disciples told [Thomas], "We have seen the Lord." But he said to them, "Unless I see the mark of the nails in his hands, and put my finger in the mark of the nails and my hand in his side, I will not believe."

A week later his disciples were again in the house, and Thomas was with them. Although the doors were shut, Jesus came and stood among them and said, "Peace be with you." Then he said to Thomas, "Put your finger here and see my hands. Reach out your hand and put it in my side. Do not doubt but believe." Thomas answered him, "My Lord and my God!" (John 20:25-28)

Considering

Our hands are incredibly complex. There are, for example, twenty-seven bones in the hand. The human hand is more complex than those of other primates chiefly because of our opposable thumb, which allows us an amazing degree of flexibility and precision. Besides constructing everything from skyscrapers and other enormous structures to tiny micro-electronics and everything in between with our hands, consider what else hands are used for every day: holding other hands or shaking them, saluting and helping pledge allegiance, helping swear an oath, pointing, drawing, shaping pottery, cooking and baking, doing amazing kinds of surgery and other healing care, directing traffic, saving lives, playing music, and communicating in countless ways—especially in sign language for those who cannot hear.

From the moment of our birth our hands are designed with fingerprints which are different from any other person ever on the earth and remain unchanged and uniquely ours throughout our lives. Our hands are indeed miracles that are right before our eyes every day.

Responding

The Old Testament book of Sirach has some important wisdom for us when we think about responding to how generous God's "hand" has been in our lives: "Do not let your hand be stretched out to receive and closed when it is time to give" (Sirach 4:31).

And later the author of Sirach elaborates further:

> Stretch out your hand to the poor, so that your blessing may be complete. Give graciously to all the living; do not withhold kindness even from the dead. Do not avoid those who weep, but mourn with those who mourn. Do not hesitate to visit the sick, because for such deeds you will be loved. (Sirach 7:32-35)

What are some of the ways that I can open my hands and "lend a hand" to others around me who could use a bit of the generosity God has so often lavished on me? It could take the shape of some actual help with tasks or some gift of food or presence, or it may even be the gift of some encouragement to someone around me who may not see his or her own goodness the way I do.

Whatever I decide, Matthew's gospel reminds me that when being generous, I don't need to make a big deal of it:

> " . . . whenever you give alms, do not sound a trumpet before you, as the hypocrites do in the synagogues and in the streets, so that they may be praised by others. Truly I tell you, they have received their reward. But when you give alms, do not let your left hand know

what your right hand is doing, so that your alms may be done in secret; and your Father who sees in secret will reward you." (Matthew 6:2-4)

Loving God, whose "hands" are so open to support and love me and all of creation, help me to learn to give with just a bit of the lavish generosity and grace that you shower on me. Thank you for the amazing gift of hands, and please bless those in a special way who do not have the use of one or both hands. Amen.

Comb or Brush:
Every Hair of My Head

Materials at hand: A comb or brush that you use (or some of your hair from it), with a candle as a prayer focus.

Centering

(Light the candle and with your hands spread open say:)
Loving God, Creator of all that is,
here I am—today, in this place,
with all the senses you have given me.
Help me to use them to come to experience you more deeply.
You are present everywhere around me;
open me to know more of the many ways
that your goodness surrounds me.
Thank you for this time to be with you and to listen to you.
Amen.

Savoring

Take a look at your comb or brush and see what you use daily as if for the first time. This tool helps you to put your hair in order as you begin your day; it works with many hairs—too many to count—helping each one to have a place and a role on your head.

Feel the shape of it and imagine yourself to be one of those hairs that it helps put in place as it goes by. Slowly draw it through your hair and be aware of how your scalp feels, noticing in a way you usually never take time for. As you do, be grateful for each of those hairs and for the gift of hair, which protects our heads and gives us a chance to express ourselves in the way we wear it.

Listening

Listen to and reflect on one or more of these passages as you watch the candlelight play across the comb or brush:

"Are not five sparrows sold for two pennies? Yet not one of them is forgotten in God's sight. But even the hairs of your head are all counted. Do not be afraid; you are of more value than many sparrows." (Luke 12:6-7)

*

[God says:] Hear me, O house of Jacob, all who remain of the house of Israel, My burden since your birth, whom I have carried from your infancy. Even to your old age I am the same, even when your hair is gray I will bear you; It is I who have done this, I who will continue, and I who will carry you to safety. (Isaiah 46:3-4, NAB)

*

O God, from my youth you have taught me, and I still proclaim your wondrous deeds. So even to old age and gray hairs, O God, do not forsake me, until I proclaim your might to all the generations to come. Your power and your righteousness, O God, reach the high heavens. You who have done great things, O God, who is like you? (Psalm 71:17-19)

*

. . . a woman in the city, who was a sinner, having learned that he was eating in the Pharisee's house, brought an alabaster jar of ointment. She stood behind [Jesus] at his feet, weeping, and began to bathe his feet with her tears and to dry them with her hair. Then she continued kissing his feet and anointing them with the ointment. . . . And he said to the woman, "Your faith has saved you; go in peace." (Luke 7:37-38, 50)

Considering

Hair is an outgrowth of our skin. All mammals have hair in some form or other, from fur to wool to bristles or quills. Our hair begins to form even before we are born, while we are still in the uterus. It is strongly affected by heredity and is usually linked to our particular ethnic background. Each hair carries the unique genetic information of our DNA, and each person's hair is different from the hair on anyone else's head.

Our hair grows from tiny follicles in the skin where the root of each hair is located, and each root in turn has a small muscle attached to it which is activated when our hair "stands on end" in an unusual situation. Most people's hair will turn gray as they age, as some of the pigment is lost from the hair shaft.

Hair is an important way for most individuals to express themselves. Think of the varieties of length and shape of hairstyles, of colorings—both natural and artificial—of decorations and wigs and hairpieces, both ones that you have seen and those throughout various parts of the world and of history. Women are often more concerned about the appearance of their hair than men—but not always.

Hair is a wonderful, glorious part of our bodies, both practical and decorative—and an amazing gift from God. If you had to guess how many hairs you had—even just on your head—what would you say? Each of them is a part of us and part of the person uniquely loved by God.

Responding

It is easy for most of us to take the gift of hair for granted. Although loss of hair or baldness may be a result of aging for some men (and occasionally women), it can also be a distressing effect of certain illnesses, especially those with high fevers, and of treatments for some illnesses such as radiation or chemotherapy for cancer. Who do I know who is facing or has faced this prospect? Can I visit them or drop them a note?

God who knows every hair on our heads, please bless all cancer patients and others experiencing a loss of hair, as well as those facing other challenges of aging besides graying hair. Please bless also those barbers and hairstylists who work hard every day to keep our hair looking its best, and thank you for the gift of hair, its wonderful variety and its beauty. When I comb or brush my hair, help me to remember how completely you love me. Amen.

Underwear: Celebrating the Body

Materials at hand: A couple items of underwear, with a candle as a prayer focus.

Centering

(Light the candle and with your hands spread open say:)
Loving God, Creator of all that is,
here I am—today, in this place,
with all the senses you have given me.
Help me to use them to come to experience you more deeply.
You are present everywhere around me;
open me to know more of the many ways
that your goodness surrounds me.
Thank you for this time to be with you and to listen to you.
Amen.

Savoring

See the garments before you first as pieces of cloth and notice their texture. Touch them, first with eyes closed and then with sight and touch combined. Smell them, knowing that besides the smell of laundry detergent your underclothes probably hold your own distinctive smell, a smell which usually only other people can detect. (This smell left in clothes is often comforting to family members after a loved one's death.)

As you imagine these undergarments covering your body, remind yourself that these parts of your body are holy because they are made by God, just as every other part of your body is, and ask God to help you appreciate every part of your body, including your genitals, more completely.

Listening

Listen to and reflect on one or more of these passages as you watch the candlelight play across the underwear before you:

Indeed, the body does not consist of one member but of many. . . . If the whole body were an eye, where would the hearing be? If the whole body were hearing, where would the sense of smell be? . . . As it is, there are many members, yet one body. The eye cannot say to the hand, "I have no need of you," nor again the head to the feet, "I have no need of you." On the contrary, the members of the body that seem to be weaker are indispensable, and those members of the body that we think less honorable we clothe with greater honor, and our less respectable members are treated with greater respect; whereas our more respectable members do not need this. But God has so arranged the body, giving the greater honor to the inferior member, that there may be no dissension within the body, but the members may have the same care for one another. (1 Corinthians 12:14, 17, 20-25)

*

. . . do you not know that your body is a temple of the Holy Spirit within you, which you have from God, and that you are not your own? For you were bought with a price; therefore glorify God in your body. (1 Corinthians 6:19-20)

*

Better off poor, healthy, and fit than rich and afflicted in body. Health and fitness are better than any gold, and a robust body than countless riches. There is no wealth better than health of body, and no gladness above joy of heart. (Sirach 30:14-16)

*

Thus said the LORD to me, "Go and buy yourself a linen loincloth, and put it on your loins, but do not dip it in water." So I bought a loincloth according to the word of the LORD, and put it on my loins. And the word of the LORD came to me a second time, saying, "Take the loincloth that you bought and are wearing, and go now to the Euphrates, and hide it there in a cleft of the rock." So I went, and hid it by the Euphrates, as the LORD commanded me. And after many days the LORD said to me, "Go now to the Euphrates, and take from there the loincloth that I commanded you to hide there." Then I went to the Euphrates, and dug, and I took the loincloth from the place where I had hidden it. But now the loincloth was ruined; it was good for nothing.

Then the word of the LORD came to me: Thus says the LORD: Just so I will ruin the pride of Judah and the great pride of Jerusalem. This evil people, who refuse to hear my words, who stubbornly follow their own will and have gone after other gods to serve them and worship them, shall be like this loincloth, which is good for nothing. For as the loincloth clings to one's loins, so I made the whole house of Israel and the whole house of Judah cling to me, says the LORD, in order that they might be for me a people, a name, a praise, and a glory. But they would not listen. (Jeremiah 13:1-11)

Considering

Our undergarments, the pieces of clothing worn closest to the skin, are not something we usually take much time to consider. In fact, at times our bodies and topics connected to our bodies, such as health, nutrition, exercise, and especially sexuality, can be awkward, rarely discussed topics in our culture. Sexuality and bodily functions such as elimination often end up as the focus of jokes, as "bathroom humor." Some cultures of the world seem to be better than ours is in dealing with our bodies, but in general we are not all that comfortable with underwear and the areas they cover.

We don't know a lot about the way undergarments have evolved in human societies, but there are only a couple times that underwear is mentioned in the Bible. One specifies that the priests of the line of Aaron needed to wear special clothes, including linen undergarments, to be pure and holy for offering sacrifice to God for the Jewish people. Evidently, wearing special underwear helped make them holy and purified for this task.

The other passage is a symbolic action on the part of the prophet Jeremiah, who uses dirty underwear, of all things, to talk about Israel's relationship with God. After the prophet has worn the loincloth and never washed it, especially after he has hidden it away for a while as he was told to, he sees that the loincloth is worthless, as are the people of Israel, who have been unfaithful. But Jeremiah also uses the image positively; God reminds us that we are as close to

Underwear: Celebrating the Body

God as our underwear is to our bodies—an interesting image, to say the least!

Responding

Our bodies are indeed wonderful and complex gifts from God, especially our sexuality, which is God-given energy for intimacy. In the first chapter of Genesis we read how our sexuality is a clear and important part of how we are made in the image of God: "So God created humankind in his image, in the image of God he created them; male and female he created them" (Genesis 1:27).

Loving God, help me to appreciate my body and my sexuality more. Help me to care well for my body, with good nutrition and a healthy amount of exercise. Please bless all those who work to keep our bodies healthy and strong, especially those in the medical and rehabilitation fields. Thank you for giving each of us just the body you wanted us to have.

Please help those in our culture who are victims of unhealthy attitudes toward sexuality, especially through sexual abuse, rape, prostitution, or pornography. And help us all to have a better understanding and more balanced respect for the goodness and beauty of your gift of sexuality, to be able to see it not as dirty or something to be ashamed of, but also not to overemphasize it. And help me remember to give thanks for a healthy body whenever I put on my underwear. Amen.

Shoe: This Is Holy Ground

Materials at hand: Any kind of shoe, with a candle as a prayer focus.

Centering

(Light the candle and with your hands spread open say:)
Loving God, Creator of all that is,
here I am—today, in this place,
with all the senses you have given me.
Help me to use them to come to experience you more deeply.
You are present everywhere around me;
open me to know more of the many ways
that your goodness surrounds me.
Thank you for this time to be with you and to listen to you.
Amen.

Savoring

Take a look at the shoe before you, for a moment pretending that you've never seen it before. What would you be able to tell about this shoe and the person who wears it if you came across it someplace? Take a look at the material(s) that the shoe is made of, predicting how it will feel before touching it.

Then touch the shoe, examining it closely inside and out with your fingers, perhaps noticing elements of the shoe that you usually miss as you put it on your foot, if the shoe is yours. Notice how the shoe is designed to fit the foot, to cover and cradle it in a way that is comfortable but also pleasant to look at. (If you think it's safe for your nose, go ahead and smell the shoe to get more information from yet another sense.)

Take some time to consider where this shoe has gone—and if it is yours, where it has taken you. Then consider where its "brother and sister" pairs of shoes have taken you—to work or school, shopping, perhaps exercising, to see friends or even to travel, many places on the journey of your life so far.

This shoe—and the foot it fits—are an important part of this journey, hopefully a journey of coming closer to God.

Listening

Listen to and reflect on one or more of these passages as you watch the candlelight play across the shoe:

> Our steps are made firm by the LORD, when he delights in our way; though we stumble, we shall not fall headlong, for the LORD holds us by the hand. (Psalm 37:23-24)
>
> *
>
> Moses was keeping the flock of his father-in-law Jethro, the priest of Midian; he led his flock beyond the wilderness, and came to Horeb, the mountain of God. There the angel of the LORD appeared to him in a flame of fire out of a bush; he looked, and the bush was blazing, yet it was not consumed. Then Moses said, "I must turn aside and look at this great sight, and see why the bush is not burned up." When the LORD saw that he had turned aside to see, God called to him out of the bush, "Moses, Moses!" And he said, "Here I am." Then he said, "Come no closer! Remove the sandals from your feet, for the place on which you are standing is holy ground." (Exodus 3:1-5)
>
> *
>
> Your word is a lamp to my feet and a light to my path. (Psalm 119:105)
>
> *
>
> [During supper Jesus] got up from the table, took off his outer robe, and tied a towel around himself. Then he poured water into a basin and began to wash the disciples' feet and to wipe them with the towel that was tied around him. . . . After he had washed their feet, had put on his robe, and had returned to the table, he said to them, "Do you know what I have done to you? You call me Teacher

and Lord—and you are right, for that is what I am. So if I, your Lord and Teacher, have washed your feet, you also ought to wash one another's feet. For I have set you an example, that you also should do as I have done to you. (John 13:4-5, 12-15)

*

The LORD is my shepherd, I shall not want. . . . He leads me in right paths for his name's sake. Even though I walk through the darkest valley, I fear no evil; for you are with me; your rod and your staff—they comfort me. (Psalm 23:1, 3-4)

*

. . . those who wait for the LORD shall renew their strength, they shall mount up with wings like eagles, they shall run and not be weary, they shall walk and not faint. (Isaiah 40:31)

Considering

Shoes come in all shapes and sizes—including moccasins, boots, sandals, wooden clogs, booties, sneakers, high heels, and slippers. They have been around for most of human history, although they were often a luxury, meant for only the rich, especially in warmer climates.

For the Jewish and early Christian culture, shoes meant sandals, which were usually taken off when entering a house, and a part of basic hospitality was washing the dusty feet of one's guests, often done by one of the household servants.

Our feet, which are often protected by shoes and so useful to our bodies, are easy to take for granted, but when we push them too far or injure them, they remind us quickly of their importance. The twenty-six bones in our feet do many kinds of work, from walking and running to kicking and jumping, skiing and skating, climbing and pedaling.

Responding

An important phrase in the Old Testament is "walking in the way of the Lord." For example, Joshua reminds the Jewish tribes:

"Take good care to observe the commandment and instruction that Moses the servant of the LORD commanded you, to love the LORD your God, to walk in all his ways, to keep his commandments, and to hold fast

Shoe: This Is Holy Ground

to him, and to serve him with all your heart and with all your soul." (Joshua 22:5)

But what, specifically, does it mean to "walk in the way of the Lord"? The prophet Micah gives us a clear idea. "He has told you, O mortal, what is good; and what does the LORD require of you but to do justice, and to love kindness, and to walk humbly with your God?" (Micah 6:8).

Am I "walking in the way of the Lord"? Where *is* the journey of my life headed? Am I treating those around me justly and kindly? Are there some ways that I could "correct my direction" but just have been too busy or too lazy to do so? I listen to the book of Proverbs as it encourages us to "change our ways":

> Put away from you crooked speech, and put devious talk far from you. Let your eyes look directly forward, and your gaze be straight before you. Keep straight the path of your feet, and all your ways will be sure. Do not swerve to the right or to the left; turn your foot away from evil. (Proverbs 4:24-27)

Correcting my "direction" and putting my life on the "straight and narrow" doesn't necessarily mean having less fun; it may actually mean using my feet to play and "skip" a bit—and perhaps getting more exercise than I was before.

God of all my steps and my whole journey, please bless all those who don't have any shoes and those who cannot walk, due to disability, age, or ill health. Bless those throughout the world who help make, sell, or repair shoes for others and bless the athletes whose shoes allow them to play well. Please show me the way to walk toward you in my life, and help us all to make better "steps" toward peace with each other. Amen.

> Teach me your way, O LORD, that I may walk in your truth; give me an undivided heart to revere your name.
>
> —PSALM 86:11

SAVORING GOD

Bed or Pillow: At Rest in God

Materials at hand: Sit by, or lie on, your bed (or use a pillow to remind you of it), with a candle as a prayer focus.

Centering
(Light the candle and with your hands spread open say:)
Loving God, Creator of all that is,
here I am—today, in this place,
with all the senses you have given me.
Help me to use them to come to experience you more deeply.
You are present everywhere around me;
open me to know more of the many ways
that your goodness surrounds me.
Thank you for this time to be with you and to listen to you.
Amen.

Savoring
If you are sitting by—or lying on—your bed, take another look at this place where you spend about a third of your life. As your eyes sweep over the bed, try to describe, aloud or in your mind, what you see. Although we know God is everywhere, for a moment visualize God far above you, looking down on you as you lie open to God on your bed.

As you look with new eyes at the place where you take your rest, think also about the various kinds of places other people in the world lay their heads at night, from cots to cradles, hammocks to futons, to bunks or even sleeping on the ground.

88

Touch and even smell this place of renewal for you, exploring the feel of the bed in a new way. As you explore with your sense of touch, remember what it feels like to let your body begin to relax here as it does at the end of the day and its troubles float away as you drift off to sleep. (It may be tempting to take a rest right now, especially if you're lying down, but then you wouldn't have a chance to reflect on what's happening when you *do* go to sleep.)

If you have a pillow before you, look at it with care, "touching" it with your eyes. Imagine the pillow receiving your tired head and how that might feel from the pillow's perspective. Then touch the pillow, being grateful for the "support" it gives you night after night. In a sense, the pillow could say with Jesus, "Come to me, all you that are weary and are carrying heavy burdens, and I will give you rest" (Matthew 11:28).

Listening

Listen to and reflect on one or more of these passages as you watch the candlelight play across the bed or pillow:

> Because your steadfast love is better than life, my lips will praise you. . . . my mouth praises you with joyful lips when I think of you on my bed, and meditate on you in the watches of the night; for you have been my help, and in the shadow of your wings I sing for joy. (Psalm 63:3, 5-7)
>
> *
>
> . . . some men came, carrying a paralyzed man on a bed. They were trying to bring him in and lay him before Jesus; but finding no way to bring him in because of the crowd, they went up on the roof and let him down with his bed through the tiles into the middle of the crowd in front of Jesus. . . . [H]e said to the one who was paralyzed—"I say to you, stand up and take your bed and go to your home." Immediately he stood up before them, took what he had been lying on, and went to his home, glorifying God. (Luke 5:18-19, 24-25)
>
> *
>
> O Lord, God of my salvation, when, at night, I cry out in your presence, let my prayer come before you; incline your ear to my cry. (Psalm 88:1)
>
> *

Then Jesus went with them to a place called Gethsemane; and he said to his disciples, "Sit here while I go over there and pray." . . . Then he said to them, "I am deeply grieved, even to death; remain here, and stay awake with me." And going a little farther, he threw himself on the ground and prayed, "My Father, if it is possible, let this cup pass from me; yet not what I want but what you want." Then he came to the disciples and found them sleeping; and he said to Peter, "So, could you not stay awake with me one hour?" (Matthew 26:36, 38-40)

*

I lie down and sleep; I wake again, for the LORD sustains me. (Psalm 3:5)

*

Now the boy Samuel was ministering to the LORD under Eli. . . and Samuel was lying down in the temple of the LORD, where the ark of God was. Then the LORD called, "Samuel! Samuel!" and he said, "Here I am!" and ran to Eli, and said, "Here I am, for you called me." But he said, "I did not call; lie down again." So he went and lay down. The LORD called again, "Samuel!" Samuel got up and went to Eli, and said, "Here I am, for you called me." But he said, "I did not call, my son; lie down again." Now Samuel did not yet know the LORD, and the word of the LORD had not yet been revealed to him. The LORD called Samuel again, a third time. And he got up and went to Eli, and said, "Here I am, for you called me." Then Eli perceived that the LORD was calling the boy. Therefore Eli said to Samuel, "Go, lie down; and if he calls you, you shall say, 'Speak, LORD, for your servant is listening.'" So Samuel went and lay down in his place.

Now the LORD came and stood there, calling as before, "Samuel! Samuel!" And Samuel said, "Speak, for your servant is listening." (1 Samuel 3:1, 3-10)

Considering

Beds seem to have been used as early as ancient Egypt, Persia, and Babylonia, but they were only for the wealthy for much of human history. By about the sixteenth century beds became a part of middle-class homes, and gradually since then they have become a part of the lives of most people.

Night is a time for sleep, but for much of human history it was also a time of fear—as it still is at times for small children. In the past that fear was because of the complete darkness at night, a darkness we can only imagine since we live most of the time with at least some source of artificial light.

Scientists are learning much about what happens when we sleep, what helps us sleep, and the source of sleeping disorders, but most experts would agree that a good balance in our lives is one factor that seems to help us get a good night's sleep. The book of Sirach also reminds us of the importance of balance and discipline when it comes to sleep. "How ample a little is for a well-disciplined person! He does not breathe heavily when in bed. Healthy sleep depends on moderate eating; he rises early, and feels fit. The distress of sleeplessness and of nausea and colic are with the glutton" (Sirach 31:19-20).

Responding

Beds and the sleep that happens there are very important to our spirituality, especially in terms of dreams, of listening to our lives, and of the need to wake up.

There are many instances in scripture where God speaks to someone in a dream or communicates through one who can interpret dreams, including Joseph of the many-colored coat and Joseph, the spouse of Mary. Those who study dreaming and analyze dreams tell us that they are an important part of our lives that we need to honor and pay attention to.

Listening to, and reflecting on, our lives is a natural part of resting in God's love at the end of the day. I will try focusing on these questions at the end of my day: Where have I experienced God's presence the most today? Where have I experienced God's presence the least today? This practice, a form of the daily examen encouraged by St. Ignatius Loyola, the founder of the Jesuits, can be a helpful nightly spiritual discipline.

Waking up is a strong theme in many religious traditions because it is too easy for us to be walking through our days still asleep spiritually, not listening to God, as young Samuel was, or even paralyzed spiritually, like the man who was brought to Jesus.

Just as Jesus asked his disciples to stay awake with him, he asks us to stay awake to the ways that he is part of our lives. Here's how St. Paul talked about it in his letter to the Christians in Rome: ". . . [Y]ou know what time it is, how it is now the moment for you to wake from sleep. For salvation is nearer to us now than when we became believers; the night is far gone, the day is near" (Romans 13:11-12).

God of my waking and my sleeping, help me to stay awake spiritually, to listen to you in my life and in my dreams. Bless those who work at night while others are sleeping, especially nurses, emergency workers, police, and firefighters. Bless also those who make or sell beds and those who help people with sleeping disorders. Help everyone on the earth to sleep well tonight. And help me to rest peacefully in you as I crawl into bed at the end of my day. Amen.

Glasses: To See With Faith

Materials at hand: A pair of glasses (reading or sunglasses are fine), with a candle as a prayer focus.

Centering

(Light the candle and with your hands spread open say:)
Loving God, Creator of all that is,
here I am—today, in this place,
with all the senses you have given me.
Help me to use them to come to experience you more deeply.
You are present everywhere around me;
open me to know more of the many ways
that your goodness surrounds me.
Thank you for this time to be with you and to listen to you.
Amen.

Savoring

Take a look at the pair of glasses before you, there to help and/or protect the sight of the person who wears them. Follow the lines of the frames around from the end of one bow that fits around the ear to the end of the other, noticing more carefully than usual the ways in which glasses are specifically designed to fit the features of the wearer.

What kind of frames are they—metal, plastic, or a bit of both? Is the design of the frames sophisticated and cool, strictly utilitarian, or somewhere in between? What if glasses had never been invented; how would that affect you, or the wearer of the glasses, if they are not yours?

Now explore the shape of the glasses with your fingers, closing your eyes to enhance the sense of touch but being aware of their fragile nature and taking care not to touch the lenses. With your fingers find the center of the glasses that crosses the bridge of the nose. Does the design seem comfortable for the nose? If the wearer of these glasses were not able to see at all, that person would need to learn to "see" with his or her fingers instead, as you are attempting to now.

Now put the glasses on, pretending as you do that these are magical glasses which help give you the gift of wonder, of being able to marvel at what you see as though seeing it for the first time. If these are your glasses, be thankful again for what they do for your eyes; if they aren't yours, try to imagine how they are helpful to the person who usually wears them. Can you "see" what a wonderful help glasses are and what a gift the sense of sight is?

Listening

Listen to and reflect on one or more of these passages as you watch the candlelight play across the glasses:

> . . . the LORD opens the eyes of the blind. The LORD lifts up those who are bowed down; the LORD loves the righteous. (Psalm 146:8)
>
> *
>
> They came to Bethsaida. Some people brought a blind man to him and begged him to touch him. He took the blind man by the hand and led him out of the village; and when he had put saliva on his eyes and laid his hands on him, he asked him, "Can you see anything?" And the man looked up and said, "I can see people, but they look like trees, walking." Then Jesus laid his hands on his eyes again; and he looked intently and his sight was restored, and he saw everything clearly. (Mark 8:22-25)
>
> *
>
> I am the LORD, I have called you in righteousness, I have taken you by the hand and kept you; I have given you as a covenant to the people, a light to the nations, to open the eyes that are blind, to bring out the prisoners from the dungeon, from the prison those who sit in darkness. . . . I will lead the blind by a road they do not know, by paths they have not known I will guide them. I will turn the darkness before them into light, the rough places into level

ground. These are the things I will do, and I will not forsake them. . . . Listen, you that are deaf; and you that are blind, look up and see! (Isaiah 42:6-7, 16, 18)

*

As he walked along, [Jesus] saw a man blind from birth. . . . he spat on the ground and made mud with the saliva and spread the mud on the man's eyes, saying to him, "Go, wash in the pool of Siloam" (which means Sent). Then he went and washed and came back able to see. . . . [Later, Jesus] said [to him], "Do you believe in the Son of Man?" He answered, "And who is he, sir? Tell me, so that I may believe in him." Jesus said to him, "You have seen him, and the one speaking with you is he." He said, "Lord, I believe." And he worshiped him. Jesus said, "I came into this world for judgment so that those who do not see may see, and those who do see may become blind." Some of the Pharisees near him heard this and said to him, "Surely we are not blind, are we?" Jesus said to them, "If you were blind, you would not have sin. But now that you say, 'We see,' your sin remains." (John 9:1, 6-7, 35-41)

*

Say to those who are of a fearful heart, "Be strong, do not fear! Here is your God. . . . He will come and save you." Then the eyes of the blind shall be opened, and the ears of the deaf unstopped; then the lame shall leap like a deer, and the tongue of the speechless sing for joy. (Isaiah 35:4-6)

*

The hearing ear and the seeing eye—the LORD has made them both. (Proverbs 20:12)

Considering

Glasses consist of lenses or prisms worn in front of the eyes to compensate for defects of vision. For nearsightedness the lenses are concave; for farsightedness they are convex. There are often several variations even within one pair of glasses, not only because of different vision needs in each eye, but also because of use for both distance and close-up, resulting in bi- or trifocals at times. Special glasses are also used to protect eyes for safety reasons in some work environments, as well as in the sun or even under water.

Historians think glasses may have been made and worn as early as the Middle Ages, but after the invention of the printing press in the fifteenth century, there was far more demand than previously. Benjamin Franklin was the first person to wear a set of bifocals, which were made at his request.

Many people now wear contact lenses instead of glasses both for convenience and cosmetic reasons. Leonardo da Vinci suggested the possibility of contacts in 1508, but they were not actually made until the twentieth century, with modern contacts not available until the second half of the century.

We rely on our sense of sight more often than we realize, whether we wear glasses or not. We take in a great deal of information through our eyes, especially with the widespread reliance on television, computers, and video technology. In fact, we often use images from our sense of sight when we talk about knowledge and insight—as in the expression "I see what you mean"—and we also talk in terms of "blindness" at times when we're discussing ignorance or prejudice.

Responding

When it comes to having "20/20 spiritual vision," scripture reminds us of the qualities to have, including not judging others and clearly seeing the poor in our midst.

In the second letter of Peter, the author encourages his readers to work on improving their "eyesight" in faith by putting into practice what they believe:

> For this very reason, you must make every effort to support your faith with goodness, and goodness with knowledge, and knowledge with self-control, and self-control with endurance, and endurance with god-liness, and godliness with mutual affection, and mutual affection with love. For if these things are yours and are increasing among you, they keep you from being ineffective and unfruitful in the knowledge of our Lord Jesus Christ. For anyone who lacks these things is near-sighted and blind, and is forgetful of the cleansing of past sins. (2 Peter 1:5-9)

Jesus also reminds us how useless it is to judge others and to decide what they need to do differently when we have so much to work on in our own lives first, and he does this by using a strong visual image: "Why do you see the speck in your neighbor's eye, but do not notice the log in your own eye? Or how can you say to your neighbor, 'Let me take the speck out of your eye,' while the log is in your own eye? You hypocrite, first take the log out of your own eye, and then you will see clearly to take the speck out of your neighbor's eye" (Matthew 7:3-5).

Who is the person in my life that I waste energy judging when I should be thinking about what I need to change in *myself*? How can I work on not judging this person?

One aspect of our lives that it is easy to be "blind" to is the poor among us, whether the homeless, the hungry, or the unemployed. The book of Sirach reminds us to look again at the needs of the poor:

> My child, do not cheat the poor of their living, and do not keep needy eyes waiting. Do not grieve the hungry, or anger one in need. Do not add to the troubles of the desperate, or delay giving to the needy. Do not reject a suppliant in distress, or turn your face away from the poor. Do not avert your eye from the needy . . . . (Sirach 4:1-5)

Where are the places in my life that I can give to the poor who are close at hand? Is there a container for the food bank at my local store? Is there a food or clothing drive coming up that I can help with or give to? Is there someone in need of my company or time in my neighborhood or among my friends? Help me to "see" the needs before me, loving God.

God of all that is seen and unseen, bless those who have lost, or are losing, their eyesight, and bless all those who help them. Bless those who wear contacts and glasses and the professionals who help all those with eye and vision problems. Bless, too, those who work with special kinds of "glasses" and lenses, from the smallest microscope to the largest telescope, as they help to increase our knowledge and awareness of the amazing world and universe around us.

Open the "eyes" of my heart to more clearly "see" you at work in my life and in others around me, especially in those in need. Amen.

Ring: Love Without End

Materials at hand: A ring, with a candle as a prayer focus.

Centering

(Light the candle and with your hands spread open say:)
Loving God, Creator of all that is,
here I am—today, in this place,
with all the senses you have given me.
Help me to use them to come to experience you more deeply.
You are present everywhere around me;
open me to know more of the many ways
that your goodness surrounds me.
Thank you for this time to be with you and to listen to you.
Amen.

Savoring

Watch the candle's light play on the ring, whether it is on the table or on your finger. Let your eye "travel" the circle of the ring, noticing any differences in the width or texture or design of the ring.

Then use your fingertips to explore it, at first with your eyes closed and then using both your fingers and your eyes. Is there anything that you hadn't noticed before, including the intricate detailing that is often present on a ring?

Put the ring on, or put it on again if you already had it on. Specifically, how does it feel different now from when you were exploring it from the outside only? How does your finger feel when surrounded by the ring?

Recall the history of this particular ring, if you know it; how do you perceive this ring differently than someone who doesn't know its history? Think about the stories this ring might tell if it could speak.

Listening

Listen to and reflect on one or more of these passages as you watch the candlelight play across the ring:

> One's almsgiving is like a signet ring with the Lord, and he will keep a person's kindness like the apple of his eye. (Sirach 17:22)
>
> *
>
> "So [the prodigal son] set off and went to his father. But while he was still far off, his father saw him and was filled with compassion; he ran and put his arms around him and kissed him. Then the son said to him, 'Father, I have sinned against heaven and before you; I am no longer worthy to be called your son.' But the father said to his slaves, 'Quickly, bring out a robe—the best one—and put it on him; put a ring on his finger and sandals on his feet. And get the fatted calf and kill it, and let us eat and celebrate; for this son of mine was dead and is alive again; he was lost and is found!' And they began to celebrate." (Luke 15:20-24)
>
> *
>
> A word fitly spoken is like apples of gold in a setting of silver. Like a gold ring or an ornament of gold is a wise rebuke to a listening ear. (Proverbs 25:11-12)

Considering

A ring is a piece of jewelry, but often so much more. It can be a symbol of engagement or marriage, as it has been especially since the fifteenth or sixteenth century. (Such rings were worn on different fingers and even the thumb at different times and in various places. One explanation for the Western custom of wearing wedding or engagement rings on the third finger of the left hand is that early theories of the circulation of the blood held that there was a direct connection between that finger and the heart, the seat of love.)

Rings have at times been a symbol of status, as they were for the Greeks and Romans. In those societies the kind of ring one wore often indicated one's rank and whether one was slave or free, a very important distinction.

The signet ring has long been a special sign of power or rank. For example, in the Old Testament both Joseph (of the many-colored coat) and Esther's cousin Mordecai were given signet rings by the Pharaoh and the king respectively, which gave them important authority and the ability to issue orders sealed with the ruler's seal.

Beginning in the Middle Ages a bishop began to receive a ring as a sign of his office. The pope also receives a "fisherman's ring," with his name inscribed around an image of Peter the fisherman, the first pope. The ring, used to seal official documents, is destroyed at his death.

Whether as a sign of friendship or love or status or power, the circular band without an end is indeed a powerful symbol.

Responding

Rings are often a sign of a covenant, a commitment to be faithful, whether in marriage or in a position of authority. Not only is God the source of all faithfulness in our lives, God has promised faithful love to Abraham and to all his descendants, including each of us: "I will establish my covenant between me and you, and your offspring after you throughout their generations, for an everlasting covenant, to be God to you and to your offspring after you" (Genesis 17:7).

The prophet Isaiah reminds us of the wonder of God's promise of faithfulness: "Have you not known? Have you not heard? The LORD is the everlasting God, the Creator of the ends of the earth. He does not faint or grow weary; his understanding is unsearchable" (Isaiah 40:28)

We know of God's tenderness, even in the face of Israel's—and our—disobedience and betrayal: "I have loved you with an everlasting love; therefore I have continued my faithfulness to you" (Jeremiah 31:3).

With a renewed appreciation for God's faithful love—that doesn't need a ring to symbolize it—I think of all those who are faithful to their commitments—to spouses or religious vows, to children, to those who are elderly and needing care, to studies or difficult jobs or other challenges. I pray for their commitment and faithfulness.

Loving God, you never give up on me; help me to be faithful to all my commitments and to you, and to remember that faithfulness whenever I see this ring. Amen.

Lotion: Anointed With Oil

Materials at hand: A bottle or container of lotion or oil, with a candle as a prayer focus.

Centering

(Light the candle and with your hands spread open say:)
Loving God, Creator of all that is,
here I am—today, in this place,
with all the senses you have given me.
Help me to use them to come to experience you more deeply.
You are present everywhere around me;
open me to know more of the many ways
that your goodness surrounds me.
Thank you for this time to be with you and to listen to you.
Amen.

Savoring

Spend a moment just looking at the bottle of lotion or oil. What is your expectation—based on the information on the container or past experience—of what the lotion or oil will feel like and what it will do to your skin? Notice any dry or rough areas on your hands or other parts of your skin. Would the moisturizing of the oil or oil-based lotion be helpful to your skin there? How do you imagine it will feel as it first goes on your skin and then as it sinks in?

Now open the container. Is there a scent? Does the scent remind you of anything? Is it pleasant to your nose or not? Now pour a very small amount onto the palm of one hand. Take a look at it as it glistens in your hand. Touch it with a finger from the other hand and notice how it feels. Spread it a little on the palm of the hand where it already is and then look at the difference between the skin that has oil or lotion and the skin that doesn't. Can you feel any difference between them?

Now gently and very slowly begin to smooth the lotion or oil onto both hands, pretending as you do that first one hand and then the other is another person smoothing the lotion on your hands, helping them to become softer and feel renewed. Notice how quickly the oil absorbs into your skin.

Now smell and carefully feel your hands (and any other skin where you put the oil or lotion). Does your skin feel and smell the way you would have expected it to? How does it feel different than it did before the lotion, if at all?

Applying oil or lotion—anointing, as it was once called—is an ancient and important act that uses many of our senses.

Listening

Listen to and reflect on one or more of these passages as you watch the candlelight play across the bottle of lotion or oil and your now-soft hands:

> The LORD spoke to Moses: Take the finest spices: of liquid myrrh five hundred shekels, and of sweet-smelling cinnamon half as much, that is, two hundred fifty, and two hundred fifty of aromatic cane, and five hundred of cassia—measured by the sanctuary shekel—and a hin of olive oil; and you shall make of these a sacred anointing oil blended as by the perfumer; it shall be a holy anointing oil. With it you shall anoint the tent of meeting and the ark of the covenant, and the table and all its utensils, and the lampstand and its utensils, and the altar of incense, and the altar of burnt offering with all its utensils, and the basin with its stand; you shall consecrate them, so that they may be most holy; whatever touches them will become holy. You shall anoint Aaron and his sons, and consecrate them, in order that they may serve me as priests. You shall say to the Israelites, "This shall be my holy anointing oil throughout your generations. It shall not be used in any ordinary anointing of the body, and you shall make no other like it in composition; it is holy, and it shall be holy to you." (Exodus 30:22-32)

*

You prepare a table before me in the presence of my enemies; you anoint my head with oil; my cup overflows. Surely goodness and mercy shall follow me all the days of my life, and I shall dwell in the house of the LORD my whole life long. (Psalm 23:5-6)

*

The LORD said to Samuel, " . . . I will send you to Jesse the Bethlehemite, for I have provided for myself a king among his sons." . . . Samuel did what the LORD commanded, and came to Bethlehem. . . . Jesse made seven of his sons pass before Samuel, and Samuel said to Jesse, "The LORD has not chosen any of these." Samuel said to Jesse, "Are all your sons here?" And he said, "There remains yet the youngest, but he is keeping the sheep." And Samuel said to Jesse, "Send and bring him; for we will not sit down until he comes here." He sent and brought him in. Now he was ruddy, and had beautiful eyes, and was handsome. The LORD said, "Rise and anoint him; for this is the one." Then Samuel took the horn of oil, and anointed him in the presence of his brothers; and the spirit of the LORD came mightily upon David from that day forward. (1 Samuel 16:1, 4, 10-13)

*

[The Lord said to Moses:] You shall take the anointing oil, and pour it on [Aaron's] head and anoint him. (Exodus 29:7)

*

One of the Pharisees asked Jesus to eat with him, and he went into the Pharisee's house and took his place at the table. And a woman in the city, who was a sinner, having learned that he was eating in the Pharisee's house, brought an alabaster jar of ointment. She stood behind him at his feet, weeping, and began to bathe his feet with her tears and to dry them with her hair. Then she continued kissing his feet and anointing them with the ointment. Now when the Pharisee who had invited him saw it, he said to himself, "If this man were a prophet, he would have known who and what kind of woman this is who is touching him—that she is a sinner." . . . [T]urning toward the woman, he said to Simon, "Do you see this woman? I entered your house; you gave me no water for my feet, but she has bathed my feet with her tears and dried them with her hair. You gave me no kiss, but from the time I came in she has not stopped kissing my feet. You did not anoint my head with oil, but she has anointed my feet with ointment. Therefore, I tell you, her sins, which were many, have been forgiven; hence she has shown great love. But the one to whom little is forgiven, loves little." Then he said to her, "Your sins are forgiven." (Luke 7:36-39, 44-48)

*

Are any among you sick? They should call for the elders of the church and have them pray over them, anointing them with oil in the name of the Lord. (James 5:14)

Considering

Olive oil, which is plentiful in the Middle East, was used for a number of purposes besides cooking and baking; among other things, it was an important source of light for lamps as well as a primitive medicine to help in healing.

It also had an important spiritual function; it was used in offering sacrifices to God, and especially when blended with spices to make it fragrant, it was used to anoint. Anointing is a practice whose exact origins are unclear but whose purpose is to help designate a person or thing as sacred, set aside, for or of God. Kings, such as David, were anointed; so were the priests of the line of Aaron. Later, the early Christians evidently anointed those who were sick in the community as they prayed for their healing. Anointing is found in the Catholic sacrament of the anointing of the sick, as well as in the sacraments of baptism, confirmation, and holy orders.

Although our climate may not usually be as hot and dry as the climate of the Middle East, we often use oil to moisturize our skin—whether because of sun or shaving or bathing—and it is found in many of the products marketed to us by the multibillion dollar cosmetics industry. Using fragrant oil for the skin is an ancient human practice; scented oils have been found in Egyptian graves dating back to 3000 B.C.

Responding

As we use oils and lotions in our lives, is there a sense in which we are "anointing" ourselves? Although it can be hard to think of ourselves as anything close to holy, there is clearly a sense in which we are indeed holy because we belong to God, who is the source of holiness. The first letter of Peter reminds us, ". . . as he who called you is holy, be holy yourselves in all your conduct; for it is written, 'You shall be holy, for I am holy'" (1 Peter 1:15-16).

If we *are* holy, that means that we are called to live differently than we would without that vision of ourselves, to be kind and accepting, for example, especially to those with whom we live and to whom we are related. Psalm 133 puts it this way: "How very good and pleasant it is when kindred live together in unity! It is like the precious oil on the head, running down upon the beard, on the beard of Aaron, running down over the collar of his robes" (Psalm 133:1-2). How can I "live in unity" by changing the way I deal with someone in my life whom I find hard to accept as she or he is?

When Jesus announced the beginning of his ministry in Luke's gospel, he read from the prophet Isaiah, who talks about what he—and all of us—are anointed to do: "The spirit of the Lord GOD is upon me, because the LORD has anointed me; he has sent me to bring good news to the oppressed, to bind up the brokenhearted, to proclaim liberty to the captives, and release to the prisoners . . ." (Isaiah 61:1). How can I be a sign of good news to those around me, to those who are brokenhearted, or those feeling captive or imprisoned? Is there someone I know who is homebound who would enjoy a visit? Or someone who may be a bit down or depressed lately that would like a call or a note?

God of ointments and oils, of all that soothes our skin, please bless all those with skin problems, from burns to acne, from eczema to leprosy (Hansen's disease). Bless those who help treat skin problems and those who work with massage and similar therapies. Also, please bless all leaders who are "anointed" to help shape the way to the future; give them the graces to do well what they have been chosen to do.

Whenever I use lotion or oil, help me to remember my own holiness because of yours and to live in the light of that holiness. Amen.

Favorite Food: Taste and See

Materials at hand: A sample of your favorite food (If you have more than one, choose one for this exercise. If it isn't possible to have it in front of you, then use a picture of it or write the name of it on a piece of paper.); a candle as a prayer focus.

Centering

(Light the candle and with your hands spread open say:)
Loving God, Creator of all that is,
here I am—today, in this place,
with all the senses you have given me.
Help me to use them to come to experience you more deeply.
You are present everywhere around me;
open me to know more of the many ways
that your goodness surrounds me.
Thank you for this time to be with you and to listen to you.
Amen.

Savoring

First, look at the food you like so well. Then close your eyes and reconstruct the appearance in your mind's eye. What are the colors and the textures involved?

Then smell it—with your eyes still closed, which allows you to focus on your sense of smell. Scientists tell us that most of what we experience as taste is really smell, so this particular sense plays more of a role than it may seem.

Next, touch your favorite food, also with your eyes closed to accentuate the information you receive through your fingertips. (If you don't have this food in front of you, you will need to have your imagination on maximum power to do these exercises.) Some foods have a far more complex texture—for example, popcorn or pizza—than others, like chocolate.

Before you taste it, consult your taste buds to predict what it will taste like from past experience. Then take a small taste and see how close you were. Take time to savor the taste. This is different from just eating; it is more like a wine taster savoring a fine wine.

Listening

Listen to and reflect on one or more of these passages as you watch the candlelight play across the rest of your favorite food and while the taste—real or imagined—plays across your taste buds:

> The eyes of all look to you, and you give them their food in due season. You open your hand, satisfying the desire of every living thing. (Psalm 145:15-16)
>
> *
>
> You cause the grass to grow for the cattle, and plants for people to use, to bring forth food from the earth, and wine to gladden the human heart, oil to make the face shine, and bread to strengthen the human heart. (Psalm 104:14-15)
>
> *
>
> On this mountain the LORD of hosts will make for all peoples a feast of rich food, a feast of well-aged wines, of rich food filled with marrow, of well-aged wines strained clear. (Isaiah 25:6)
>
> *
>
> Why do you spend your money for that which is not bread, and your labor for that which does not satisfy? Listen carefully to me, and eat what is good, and delight yourselves in rich food. Incline your ear, and come to me; listen, so that you may live. (Isaiah 55:2-3)
>
> *
>
> How sweet are your words to my taste, sweeter than honey to my mouth! (Psalm 119:103)
>
> *
>
> O taste and see that the LORD is good . . . . (Psalm 34:8)

Considering

Who knows why one person likes one food and another person something quite different. All we know is that it's a good thing that there is such a wide variety of foods for the many kinds of tastes that exist.

Food does more than nourish our bodies; it also "feeds" our souls, especially in the act of eating together. Although we may at times eat alone, eating is a naturally social act; when we eat with others, we share more than physical hunger. We share the need to be nourished by others' presence. Most cultures have a strong sense of hospitality, which inevitably involves shared food. Every human celebration also typically involves food, whether it be birthday parties, cocktail parties, or picnics.

While there is certainly a need for balance in how much we eat, one of the ways that God can communicate love and delight to each of us is through our favorite foods. The challenge is to remember what a gift food is and how fortunate we are to have all we need, which we can often lose sight of in a land of relative plenty.

Responding

The letter of James puts a challenge to us pretty bluntly: "If a brother or sister is naked and lacks daily food, and one of you says to them, 'Go in peace; keep warm and eat your fill,' and yet you do not supply their bodily needs, what is the good of that?" (James 2:15-16).

The food that I have—especially my favorite food—is indeed a gift from God, one that I work hard for, but in faith I can see that my ability to work is, in turn, a gift. It is good that I enjoy food, especially certain foods, and that I am grateful to God for what I enjoy. But part of being grateful to God is the action of sharing food with those who have much less than I do. The next time I have my favorite food, I will consider donating some money or food to the local food bank.

Jesus reminds us that in feeding the hungry we are really feeding him:

> "Then the king will say to those at his right hand,
> 'Come, you that are blessed by my Father, inherit the

kingdom prepared for you from the foundation of the world; for I was hungry and you gave me food, I was thirsty and you gave me something to drink, I was a stranger and you welcomed me. . . .'" (Matthew 25:34-35)

Loving God, help me to see this food before me and all food as a gift from you to be shared generously with others, as you share it so generously with me. Amen.

(Now enjoy the rest of your favorite food!)

Address Book:
The Grace of Friends

Materials at hand: Your address book (or a list of some of your friends' names or some of their pictures), with a candle as a prayer focus.

Centering

(Light the candle and with your hands spread open say:)
Loving God, Creator of all that is,
here I am—today, in this place,
with all the senses you have given me.
Help me to use them to come to experience you more deeply.
You are present everywhere around me;
open me to know more of the many ways
that your goodness surrounds me.
Thank you for this time to be with you and to listen to you.
Amen.

Savoring

Choose one of the names from the address book or from the list or pictures before you. Close your eyes and picture that friend, with you in a favorite place where you like to spend time together. Take note of what your friend is wearing and what he or she is doing while you spend time together.

Take this opportunity in your imagination to tell this friend what he or she means to you and how much you appreciate the ways he or she has been there for you at various times in your life. You may never have actually told this person what you are saying to him or her in your imagination now, but it's good to let those close to us know what they mean to us.

Watch yourself give that person a hug or whatever gesture would be appropriate to express your friendship with her or him. Then try to imagine your life without this person and how different you might be. The author Anais Nin wisely observed, "Each friend represents a world in us, a world possibly not born until they arrive, and it is only by this meeting that a new world is born." Friends are indeed gifts from God.

Listening

Listen to and reflect on one or more of these passages as you watch the candlelight play across the address book or list or pictures:

Happy is the one who finds a friend. . . . (Sirach 25:9)

*

"As the Father has loved me, so I have loved you; abide in my love. . . . This is my commandment, that you love one another as I have loved you. No one has greater love than this, to lay down one's life for one's friends. You are my friends if you do what I command you. I do not call you servants any longer, because the servant does not know what the master is doing; but I have called you friends, because I have made known to you everything that I have heard from my Father. You did not choose me but I chose you. . . . I am giving you these commands so that you may love one another." (John 15:9, 12-17)

*

When you gain friends, gain them through testing, and do not trust them hastily. For there are friends who are such when it suits them, but they will not stand by you in time of trouble. . . . Faithful friends are a sturdy shelter: whoever finds one has found a treasure. Faithful friends are beyond price; no amount can balance their worth. . . . Do not abandon old friends, for new ones cannot equal them. A new friend is like new wine; when it has aged, you can drink it with pleasure. (Sirach 6:7-8, 14-15; 9:10)

*

And [Jesus] said to them, "Suppose one of you has a friend, and you go to him at midnight and say to him, 'Friend, lend me three loaves of bread; for a friend of mine has arrived, and I have nothing to set before him.' And he answers from within, 'Do not bother me; the door has already been locked, and my children are with me in bed; I cannot get up and give you anything.' I tell you, even though he will not get up and give him anything because he is his friend, at least because of his persistence he will get up and give him whatever he needs.

"So I say to you, Ask, and it will be given you; search, and you will find; knock, and the door will be opened for you. For everyone who asks receives, and everyone who searches finds, and for everyone who knocks, the door will be opened." (Luke 11:5-10)

*

Some friends play at friendship but a true friend sticks closer than one's nearest kin. (Proverbs 18:24)

Considering

Each one of our friends has at least one story attached to them: the story of how we became friends. Usually, though, there are far more stories than that, stories of "Remember the time when we . . . ."

Each friendship has a uniqueness to it, not only because of the two (or more) unique individuals involved and their unique history together, but also because of the qualities of that friendship. Although there are some common themes to friendship, each relationship will show them in a somewhat different way. Friends usually have common interests, loyalty, an availability to the other, an ability to be honest with each other (and because of that to irritate the other), the willingness to forgive the other's shortcomings, a mutuality and an ability to just *be* with the other, not needing to *do* anything particular. Sometimes friends share secrets together, and sometimes not, but there is usually a strong trust that doesn't need to be spoken about or questioned. In a sense, a friend gives a place for one's soul to resonate.

Responding

Scripture reminds us of the need to forgive our friends at times, but also to use good judgment in whom we call "friend."

Because friends aren't perfect, we may let each other down at times, and that's the time not to hold a grudge, according to the book of Proverbs. "One who forgives an affront fosters friendship, but one who dwells on disputes will alienate a friend" (Proverbs 17:9). Is there anyone that I need to forgive so that our friendship can survive? How will I offer that forgiveness?

Healthy discretion in the choice of friends is also important. There are people who say they are our friends but are really far from it. Proverbs reminds us, "Wealth brings many friends, but the poor are left friendless" (Proverbs 19:4). And the book of Sirach puts it pretty directly: "Every friend says, 'I too am a friend'; but some friends are friends only in name" (Sirach 37:1). Is there anyone in my life or in someone's life that I know who seems not to be a true friend? If so, I can pray for wisdom for myself or that other person, but it's really not my place to give anyone else advice about friendships unless asked.

I will take time to call or write at least one friend—perhaps one I haven't talked to in a while—and let that person know how very special he or she is in my life.

Loving God, the deepest Friend we will ever know, thank you for the gift of friends, for the deep joy and peace that friendship can bring to our lives. Bless our friends and everyone who is a friend; keep them close and loyal and trusting so that in their love and friendship they may reflect you, because you are love, and those who abide in love abide in you, and you abide in them (1 John 4:16). Amen.

Praying With
Everyday Objects

Bread and Flour:
The Bread of Life

Materials at hand: A slice of bread and a small amount of flour, with a candle as a prayer focus.

Centering

(Light the candle and with your hands spread open say:)
Loving God, Creator of all that is,
here I am—today, in this place,
with all the senses you have given me.
Help me to use them to come to experience you more deeply.
You are present everywhere around me;
open me to know more of the many ways
that your goodness surrounds me.
Thank you for this time to be with you and to listen to you.
Amen.

Savoring

Take a look at the slice of bread, which once was primarily flour, like the small amount near it. Even before the flour went through the process of becoming bread, it first had to be ground from wheat. First, sniff and then run your fingers through the flour, a powder that looks fairly lifeless, but which we know can help sustain life and is sometimes even called the "staff of life."

In order to become the slice of bread, this flour was mixed with other ingredients, including yeast, then kneaded and allowed to rise before being baked. Touch the slice of bread and notice its soft texture and the fine holes indicating that the yeast has done its job in making the bread lighter by trapping carbon dioxide in the dough. Smell the rich result of that baking and imagine the warm, rich smell as it first came from the oven. Think of all the hands and effort that helped bring this slice of bread to your home and table.

Taste some of the slice of bread, noticing the rich combination of tastes—a bit of sweetness as well as the salt, yeast, and flour.

Listening

Listen to and reflect on one or more of these passages as you watch the candlelight play across the flour and the rest of the slice of bread:

> He told them another parable: "The kingdom of heaven is like yeast that a woman took and mixed in with three measures of flour until all of it was leavened." (Matthew 13:33)
>
> *
>
> While they were eating, Jesus took a loaf of bread, and after blessing it he broke it, gave it to the disciples, and said, "Take, eat; this is my body." (Matthew 26:26)
>
> *
>
> Jesus said to them, "I am the bread of life. Whoever comes to me will never be hungry, and whoever believes in me will never be thirsty." (John 6:35)
>
> *
>
> When he was at the table with [the two disciples from Emmaus], he took bread, blessed and broke it, and gave it to them. Then their eyes were opened, and they recognized him; and he vanished from their sight. They said to each other, "Were not our hearts burning within us while he was talking to us on the road, while he was opening the scriptures to us?" (Luke 24:30-32)
>
> *
>
> "Give us each day our daily bread." (Luke 11:3)

Considering

Bread, of one form or another, seems to have been important to the human community since prehistoric times. Today, whether it's bagels or flatbread, pasta or pocket bread, matzo or baguettes, sandwiches or tortillas, bread satisfies much of the hunger of people throughout the world every day. Breaking bread together is an important part of any act of hospitality. We even get our word "companion" from the one who breaks or shares bread (*pane*) with (*cum*) us.

We can lose sight of the gift of bread and the act of baking it when we can so easily go to the supermarket and get a loaf of bread. But for much of the world today and for most of human history bread was something precious, to be both made and shared in the home.

The Jewish festival of Passover is also called the feast of Unleavened Bread because the Jews couldn't wait for their bread to rise in their haste to escape the Pharaoh in Egypt and so had to eat their bread unleavened, on the run. The Christian eucharist began at such a Passover meal, and early Christians met in one another's homes for the "breaking of the bread," as the eucharist was first known.

To eat—or share—bread is indeed an important human and spiritual activity.

Responding

In Paul's first letter to the Christians in Corinth, he talks about the implications of sharing bread: "Because there is one bread, we who are many are one body, for we all partake of the one bread" (1 Corinthians 10:17).

And the book of Proverbs reminds us, "Those who are generous are blessed, for they share their bread with the poor" (Proverbs 22:9).

Is there someone I know who would like some bread or—perhaps even more—a chance to "share bread" with me? Perhaps it's a lonely neighbor or a friend whom I haven't talked to in a while. Can I find time to have lunch, or even coffee, with that person?

Or maybe I can donate to, or get involved with, an organization like Bread for the World, seeking justice for the world's hungry people through lobbying.

Bread baker God, help me to see what a gift my daily bread is— whether sandwich, toast, or donut—and to share with others what you have so generously shared with me. Amen.

Bread and Flour: The Bread of Life

Salt: You Are the Salt of the Earth

Materials at hand: A salt shaker or any container of salt, with a candle as a prayer focus.

Centering

(Light the candle and with your hands spread open say:)
Loving God, Creator of all that is,
here I am—today, in this place,
with all the senses you have given me.
Help me to use them to come to experience you more deeply.
You are present everywhere around me;
open me to know more of the many ways
that your goodness surrounds me.
Thank you for this time to be with you and to listen to you.
Amen.

Savoring

Look at the salt shaker or the container the salt is in. Try to predict how many grains of salt there might be in that container and to imagine what the salt tastes like.

Then shake a little bit into your hand or onto a plate. Take a look at how small the grains of salt are and how they sparkle in the light if you move your hand or the plate around. The sparkling is the light reflecting off the flat sides of the nearly-perfectly cubic salt crystals.

Does the salt have a smell?

Now for a taste: moisten your finger, touch it to the salt, and then take a little taste of the salt. Pay attention to whether the taste changes as the saltiness hits different parts of your tongue. How long does it take before the salty taste is basically gone?

Salt is such a simple, daily substance, but it is important to us in a surprising number of ways.

Listening

Listen to and reflect on one or more of these passages as you watch the candlelight play across the salt and salt shaker:

> [Jesus said to the disciples,] "You are the salt of the earth; but if salt has lost its taste, how can its saltiness be restored? It is no longer good for anything, but is thrown out and trampled under foot.
>
> "You are the light of the world. A city built on a hill cannot be hid. No one after lighting a lamp puts it under the bushel basket, but on the lampstand, and it gives light to all in the house. In the same way, let your light shine before others, so that they may see your good works and give glory to your Father in heaven." (Matthew 5:13-16)
>
> *
>
> [The Lord spoke to Aaron:] All the holy offerings that the Israelites present to the LORD I have given to you, together with your sons and daughters, as a perpetual due; it is a covenant of salt forever before the LORD for you and your descendants as well. (Numbers 18:19)

Considering

Salt—sodium chloride (formula: NaCl)—is a simple chemical compound, but it is essential to our bodies' functions and widely distributed throughout nature. As an electrolyte, salt helps our kidneys regulate the body's fluid levels and their acidity. We need a certain amount of it in our diet, although the typical diet today provides far more salt than we need. The oceans of the world are one of the places we find salt in nature; they are about three percent salt by weight, which is said to be similar to the proportion in our bodies.

Salt has been important since the earliest times, for preserving food as well as seasoning it. It was even used as currency at some points, and our word "salary" originally comes from the term for the salt allotment given regularly to Roman soldiers.

The source for salt in biblical times would have been the Dead Sea, and at one location along its shores there are huge salt formations resembling statues, which is probably where the story of Lot's wife turning into a pillar of salt (Genesis 19:26) came from. And although salt can't really lose its flavor, it can become unclean as far as Jewish practices are concerned and so would need to be thrown out.

The salt shared with the food at a banquet in Jewish life was an important symbol of the bond of friendship and solidarity, of a covenant of friendship, and salt was also an important part of the ritual offerings made to God in the Old Testament.

Salt is indeed an important part of our lives—and you don't need to take that with a grain of salt!

Responding

In St. Paul's Letter to the Colossians, along with some other advice to that community, he adds, "Let your speech always be gracious, seasoned with salt, so that you may know how you ought to answer everyone" (Colossians 4:6).

How do I "season" my life? Is there any "bitterness" in my life? Am I "sweet" to others and kind in the way I treat them? Is my life pretty "bland" and lifeless when it comes to how I live out my faith? Or is there a "tang" evident of what is really important to me: my relationship with God?

What can I do to "adjust the seasonings"? I will think of one action that would better reflect what I believe in the way I act toward others, such as telling those I love how much they mean to me more often.

God of all the elements, "season" me with your love so that the "flavor" of it is clear to all those I meet. Please bless all those who work to provide salt and all the seasonings we so easily take for granted. Amen.

Salt: You Are the Salt of the Earth

Facial Tissues: To You I Cry

Materials at hand: A couple facial tissues (or a handkerchief, if you prefer), with a candle as a prayer focus.

Centering
(Light the candle and with your hands spread open say:)
Loving God, Creator of all that is,
here I am—today, in this place,
with all the senses you have given me.
Help me to use them to come to experience you more deeply.
You are present everywhere around me;
open me to know more of the many ways
that your goodness surrounds me.
Thank you for this time to be with you and to listen to you.
Amen.

Savoring
Look at how the light from the candle and any other light plays across the folds of the tissues while they are lying before you, and try to predict what your fingers will feel as you touch them. Now pick one up, closing your eyes to concentrate on what your fingers can tell you. Notice its texture, which is an interesting combination of softness and strength.

Use your nose; is there a scent?

Now use your ears; a tissue makes a surprising amount of noise if you crinkle it.

Open your eyes and let the tissue cover the palm of your hand. Think of all the ways you have used tissues throughout your life.

Think of all the colds and sneezes—and all the tears of disappointment and pain and frustration and perhaps anger that have been a part of your life. (This may take quite a bit of time to recall; give yourself all the time you need.)

Let your imagination lay all that now in the center of this tissue as you offer all those experiences to God as prayers of the heart. A tissue is such a common object that we can easily take it for granted, but others like this one have perhaps watched our deepest self unfold.

Listening

Listen to and reflect on one or more of these passages as you watch the candlelight play across the tissues:

> For everything there is a season, and a time for every matter under heaven: a time to be born, and a time to die; a time to plant, and a time to pluck up what is planted; a time to kill, and a time to heal; a time to break down, and a time to build up; a time to weep, and a time to laugh; a time to mourn, and a time to dance. . . . (Ecclesiastes 3:1-4)
>
> *
>
> When Jesus saw [Lazarus's sister Mary] weeping, and the Jews who came with her also weeping, he was greatly disturbed in spirit and deeply moved. He said, "Where have you laid him?" They said to him, "Lord, come and see." Jesus began to weep. So the Jews said, "See how he loved him!" (John 11:33-36)
>
> *
>
> After a little while the bystanders came up and said to Peter, "Certainly you are also one of them, for your accent betrays you." Then he began to curse, and he swore an oath, "I do not know the man!" At that moment the cock crowed. Then Peter remembered what Jesus had said: "Before the cock crows, you will deny me three times." And he went out and wept bitterly. (Matthew 26:73-75)
>
> *
>
> I am weary with my moaning; every night I flood my bed with tears; I drench my couch with my weeping. My eyes waste away because of grief; they grow weak because of all my foes. Depart from me, all you workers of evil, for the LORD has heard the sound of my weeping. The LORD has heard my supplication; the LORD accepts my prayer. (Psalm 6:6-9)

*

But Mary [Magdalene] stood weeping outside the tomb. As she wept, she bent over to look into the tomb; and she saw two angels in white, sitting where the body of Jesus had been lying, one at the head and the other at the feet. They said to her, "Woman, why are you weeping?" She said to them, "They have taken away my Lord, and I do not know where they have laid him." When she had said this, she turned around and saw Jesus standing there, but she did not know that it was Jesus.

Jesus said to her, "Woman, why are you weeping? Whom are you looking for?" Supposing him to be the gardener, she said to him, "Sir, if you have carried him away, tell me where you have laid him, and I will take him away." Jesus said to her, "Mary!" She turned and said to him in Hebrew, "Rabbouni!" (which means Teacher). (John 20:11-16)

*

My tears have been my food day and night, while people say to me continually, "Where is your God?" These things I remember, as I pour out my soul: how I went with the throng, and led them in procession to the house of God, with glad shouts and songs of thanksgiving, a multitude keeping festival. Why are you cast down, O my soul, and why are you disquieted within me? Hope in God; for I shall again praise him, my help and my God. (Psalm 42:3-5)

Considering

Tears and crying are often seen as a source of weakness in our culture, especially for men. But, in fact, they serve an important function for us biologically, emotionally, and also spiritually.

Biologically, tears are produced by the lachrymal glands at the outside corner of each eye to help lubricate the eye and to flush away any foreign materials such as dust or hair. Each time we blink, a small amount of fluid from the gland is released to help bathe the eye.

When a person feels a strong emotion like grief or fear, the muscles around the lachrymal glands may tighten up and squeeze out more tear fluid than usual. Some people cry more easily than others, but situations of loss, such as death, divorce, depression, and even disappointment, may often bring on tears. They are a healthy way to relieve stress and help express feelings that otherwise might stay pent up in the body.

When it comes to spirituality, it's surprising how many references to tears and crying can be found in scripture, including the whole book of Lamentations, which is a set of poems of grief after the fall of Jerusalem in 587 B.C.

Feelings are certainly an important part of our prayer, and sometimes feelings which cannot be expressed in words or any other way may come out in tears. For some people, some of their best praying happens in tears.

Responding

The places where we experience tears in our lives are often places where we can learn a lot if we patiently listen to them. At times they may also be areas of our lives where we need outside help to deal with them.

The book of Ecclesiastes reminds us that there are many who experience a reason for tears each day: " . . . I saw all the oppressions that are practiced under the sun. Look, the tears of the oppressed— with no one to comfort them!" (Ecclesiastes 4:1).

And scripture also reminds us that the more we try to respond to those in need around us—whether by helping with hunger or homelessness locally or by comforting someone we know who has recently suffered a loss—the more God is open to our prayers. The prophet Isaiah puts it this way:

> Is not this the fast that I choose: to loose the bonds of injustice, to undo the thongs of the yoke, to let the oppressed go free, and to break every yoke? Is it not to share your bread with the hungry, and bring the home- less poor into your house; when you see the naked, to cover them, and not to hide yourself from your own kin? . . . Then you shall call, and the LORD will answer; you shall cry for help, and he will say, Here I am. (Isaiah 58:6-7, 9)

Comforting God, be with all those who are grieving and weeping today; help them to see you as the hope in their lives. Please bless all those who help others deal with places of pain in their lives, whether counselors, psychologists, psychiatrists, or just good friends. Give me the grace and the wisdom to be a comfort to others where I can, and help me not to be afraid to share my own tears with you at times. Amen.

Earphones: Listen When I Call

Materials at hand: A set of earphones, ear plugs, or even the receiver from a phone, with a candle as a prayer focus.

Centering

(Light the candle and with your hands spread open say:)
Loving God, Creator of all that is,
here I am—today, in this place,
with all the senses you have given me.
Help me to use them to come to experience you more deeply.
You are present everywhere around me;
open me to know more of the many ways
that your goodness surrounds me.
Thank you for this time to be with you and to listen to you.
Amen.

Savoring

Listen attentively to the sounds around you for at least a couple minutes, not trying to identify them as much as just noting their existence. Reflect on all the sources of noise in our contemporary living environment. What are your favorite sounds? Try to be specific and to recall them as specifically as possible. Do you have any least favorite sounds? If so, why? Try covering your ears with your hands or putting your fingers in your ears and notice that this doesn't keep out all the sound but merely muffles what is there.

Look at the earphones or earplugs or phone receiver before you. They offer a way to focus the sound that we hear (or don't, with the earplugs) rather than eliminating other sounds. Think about ways that they can be used constructively—to relax or to stay informed, for example—and ways that they could be used destructively—such as to tune others out.

As you look at them, try to imagine the sound dancing its way along the earphones or phone receiver into your ear and head (or being stopped at your ear by the earplugs) and play with that image a bit; sometimes the actual science involved in sound, hearing, and electronics can seem almost as magical. And our ears help make this wonder possible for us.

Listening

Listen to and reflect on one or more of these passages as you watch the candlelight play across the earphones or earplugs or telephone. (You may want to read them aloud so that you can physically hear them.)

> Give ear to my words, O Lord; give heed to my sighing. Listen to the sound of my cry, my King and my God, for to you I pray. (Psalm 5:1-2)
>
> *
>
> For just as the body is one and has many members, and all the members of the body, though many, are one body, so it is with Christ. . . . Indeed, the body does not consist of one member but of many. If the foot would say, "Because I am not a hand, I do not belong to the body," that would not make it any less a part of the body. And if the ear would say, "Because I am not an eye, I do not belong to the body," that would not make it any less a part of the body. If the whole body were an eye, where would the hearing be? If the whole body were hearing, where would the sense of smell be? . . . As it is, there are many members, yet one body. (1 Corinthians 12:12, 14-17, 20)
>
> *
>
> Incline your ear, and come to me; listen, so that you may live. I will make with you an everlasting covenant, my steadfast, sure love for David. (Isaiah 55:3)
>
> *
>
> [Jesus said to his disciples,] "The reason I speak to them in parables is that 'seeing they do not perceive, and hearing they do not listen, nor do they understand.' With them indeed is fulfilled the prophecy

of Isaiah that says: 'You will indeed listen, but never understand, and you will indeed look, but never perceive. For this people's heart has grown dull, and their ears are hard of hearing, and they have shut their eyes; so that they might not look with their eyes, and listen with their ears, and understand with their heart and turn—and I would heal them.' But blessed are your eyes, for they see, and your ears, for they hear." (Matthew 13:13-16)

*

The hearing ear and the seeing eye—the LORD has made them both. (Proverbs 20:12)

*

At that place [the prophet Elijah] came to a cave, and spent the night there. Then the word of the LORD came to him, saying . . . "Go out and stand on the mountain before the LORD, for the LORD is about to pass by." Now there was a great wind, so strong that it was splitting mountains and breaking rocks in pieces before the LORD, but the LORD was not in the wind; and after the wind an earthquake, but the LORD was not in the earthquake; and after the earthquake a fire, but the LORD was not in the fire; and after the fire a sound of sheer silence. When Elijah heard it, he wrapped his face in his mantle and went out and stood at the entrance of the cave. (1 Kings 19:9, 11-13)

Considering

Our sense of hearing is an important way for us to gain information. When something makes a vibration, whether it's the human voice, a musical instrument, or any one of a number of other sources of noise in our lives, those sound waves travel through the air (or through an earphone wire) and hit our outer ear. Then a complex set of interactions takes place within the ear and brain to allow us to hear at frequencies that can range from 15 to over 18,000 hertz, which is that many cycles per second. The speed of sound waves actually varies somewhat, depending on conditions like temperature; sound can not only travel through liquids, like water, and solids, it can travel faster than it travels through air.

When it comes to coping with unwanted sounds and noise, our ears don't come with lids as our eyes do. In order to survive in the noisy world in which we live, we try to "tune out" much of the sound around us, an activity that takes more energy than we sometimes realize. Watch your body relax, for example, after you hear some heavy machinery outside or a loud fan stop.

Listening for the important sounds in our lives—like the silent sound of God which the prophet Elijah knew when he heard it—becomes more difficult, the noisier our world and our lives become.

Responding

Listening to God and to others in our lives *is* hard work, because we need to set aside our own interior "static" as well as the noise from outside us.

Scripture encourages us to really listen in order to gain wisdom. The book of Proverbs urges us, "Listen to advice and accept instruction, that you may gain wisdom for the future" (Proverbs 19:20). And the book of Sirach puts it this way: "If you love to listen you will gain knowledge, and if you pay attention you will become wise. Stand in the company of the elders. Who is wise? Attach yourself to such a one" (Sirach 6:33-34). Who is there in my life whom I need to spend more time listening to? Perhaps it's an older relative or neighbor, or perhaps it's someone I know who needs a listener as much as I need to hear what he or she has to say.

One of the "voices" not heard much in our society is that of the poor. The book of Proverbs reminds us, "If you close your ear to the cry of the poor, you will cry out and not be heard" (Proverbs 21:13). How can I help the cry of the poor, whether homeless or hungry, to be heard better in my community? Can I write a letter to the editor or sign a petition for better low-income housing options? Or what?

Loving God of all sounds and all hearing, bless all those who make sounds, especially children just learning to talk and musicians. Bless all those who are hearing impaired and need hearing aids and those who help others to improve their hearing.

Please help me to take time to listen better to you, to my own life, and to others in my life—to really take what I hear to heart rather than just take it in—even at times when what I hear may be uncomfortable or not what I expected. Thank you for the gift of sound and the gift of hearing. Amen.

Pen and Paper:
You Are Our Letter

Materials at hand: A pen and some paper (plain or lined), with a candle as a prayer focus.

Centering

(Light the candle and with your hands spread open say:)
Loving God, Creator of all that is,
here I am—today, in this place,
with all the senses you have given me.
Help me to use them to come to experience you more deeply.
You are present everywhere around me;
open me to know more of the many ways
that your goodness surrounds me.
Thank you for this time to be with you and to listen to you.
Amen.

Savoring

Take a look at the pen, ready and waiting to write whatever you decide on the paper—words, thoughts, or drawings. Consider, however, that in order to understand much of what you might put there, one would need to know not only how to read but also how to read your particular language and your own handwriting.

Examine the pen as though you had never seen one before, taking careful note about how the ink gets to the point, how the point retracts—if it does, how the pen fits in your hand, and its shape, material, and weight. How might you hold this pen if you didn't already know how?

Carefully look at the paper, getting as close to the surface of it as you can so that you can look at it from a different point of view than usual. Before touching it, predict what your fingers will experience. Is there any distinctive texture to this paper? Any scent? Any color or tint? If you had never seen or felt paper before, what would you think it was made of? Would you then be surprised that it could bend and fold?

Taking the pen in your hand, now with your eyes closed, try to be as loose and relaxed as possible and write, draw, or doodle whatever comes into your head. Then take a look at what you have done, all thanks to a technology so common that we use it every day without a second thought.

Listening

Listen to and reflect on one or more of these passages as you watch the candlelight play across the pen and paper:

> Although I have much to write to you, I would rather not use paper and ink; instead I hope to come to you and talk with you face to face, so that our joy may be complete. (2 John 1:12)
>
> *
>
> The days are surely coming, says the LORD, when I will make a new covenant with the house of Israel and the house of Judah. . . . I will put my law within them, and I will write it on their hearts; and I will be their God, and they shall be my people. (Jeremiah 31:31, 33)
>
> *
>
> [T]hey crucified him, and with him two others, one on either side, with Jesus between them. Pilate . . . had an inscription written and put on the cross. It read, "Jesus of Nazareth, the King of the Jews." Many of the Jews read this inscription, because the place where Jesus was crucified was near the city; and it was written in Hebrew, in Latin, and in Greek. Then the chief priests of the Jews said to Pilate, "Do not write, 'The King of the Jews,' but, 'This man said, I am King of the Jews.'" Pilate answered, "What I have written I have written." (John 19:18-22)
>
> *
>
> Hear, O Israel: The LORD is our God, the LORD alone. You shall love the LORD your God with all your heart, and with all your soul, and with all your might. Keep these words that I am commanding

you today in your heart. Recite them to your children and talk about them when you are at home and when you are away, when you lie down and when you rise. Bind them as a sign on your hand, fix them as an emblem on your forehead, and write them on the doorposts of your house and on your gates. (Deuteronomy 6:4-9)

*

You yourselves are our letter, written on our hearts, to be known and read by all; and you show that you are a letter of Christ, prepared by us, written not with ink but with the Spirit of the living God, not on tablets of stone but on tablets of human hearts. (2 Corinthians 3:2-3)

Considering

Throughout human history both writing instruments and the surface for writing have changed a great deal. Scholars tell us that the earliest form of Western writing was cuneiform, where wedge-shaped marks were pressed into wet clay and then the clay was baked so that the marks were permanent. The early Greeks used both brushes on pottery and mallet and chisel on stone for their writing, while the Romans often used pointed styluses on wax-covered wooden tablets or carefully cut reeds on papyrus and later parchment and vellum.

Gradually through the first millennium quill pens made from the wing feathers of certain birds sharpened to a fine point were substituted for reeds as writing instruments, and they were in turn replaced by metal writing points, which became common by the nineteenth century. Fountain pens followed in the late nineteenth century, ballpoint pens after World War II, and fiber-tip pens were developed more recently.

Paper as we know it didn't exist in the West until after the year 1000, although it had been first made by a eunuch in the Chinese court in the year 150, using bark from a mulberry tree. Papyrus, originating in Egypt, was used from the fourth or fifth century B.C. until the fourth century A.D.; after that time parchment was more commonly used. Parchment, made from specially prepared and untanned hides of sheep, calves, or goats, was used for many centuries and is occasionally used today for formal honorary documents. Paper—which is really thin sheets of compressed vegetable cellulose fibers—gradually became more common, especially after the invention of the printing press in the fifteenth century, but it was usually made from rags until the nineteenth century, when the use of wood fibers was perfected.

Both pen and paper have gone through many tranformations to give us the reliable and efficient tools for writing that we have today. Despite technological changes like telephones and e-mail, pen and paper retain an important role in our lives.

Responding

In the course of my day I use a pen and paper in many ways, from to-do lists to signing checks or credit card slips to filling out forms or writing a note to a friend. Please help me see that everything I write will be true, fair, and caring.

God of all writing and communication, thank you for the gift of being able to write and to express myself on paper. Bless all those who use pens and paper in their daily work, including students, and bless those who teach others to read and write. Bless, too, all those who make and sell paper and pens of all kinds. Bless especially those who, due to distance, are able to stay in touch with friends or family only through letters and e-mail; bring them together safely with those they love. And bless those who may draw close to you through journaling about their lives.

Loving God, "write" your love "indelibly" on my heart so that I never forget you in my life, and help me to remember your love whenever I use a pen. Amen.

Keys: The Power of God

Materials at hand: A set of keys (preferably not a remote control lock, although it can be used), with a candle as a prayer focus.

Centering

(Light the candle and with your hands spread open say:)
Loving God, Creator of all that is,
here I am—today, in this place,
with all the senses you have given me.
Help me to use them to come to experience you more deeply.
You are present everywhere around me;
open me to know more of the many ways
that your goodness surrounds me.
Thank you for this time to be with you and to listen to you.
Amen.

Savoring

Set the keys before you and look at them, at first not identifying which key goes to what. Look at them as though you'd never seen them before and never even seen keys before. What a strange assortment of pieces of metal of various shapes and sizes, with a common ring to tie them together! Notice whether the keys are worn or fairly new and shiny, and explore the differences in finishes and size between them. Feel them with your fingers very carefully, first with your eyes closed and then with fingers and eyes, and hold them to your ear to hear their "music."

Now think about the purpose of each of the keys and pray about that while holding it. Pray for your house and all that happens within it while holding your house key(s), all the many ways you use your car while holding that key, about work while holding the key to there, and so forth. As you hold each key, try to picture God holding that part of your life lovingly in God's hands.

Listening

Listen to and reflect on one or more of these passages as you watch the candlelight play across the keys:

"And I tell you, you are Peter, and on this rock I will build my church, and the gates of Hades will not prevail against it. I will give you the keys of the kingdom of heaven, and whatever you bind on earth will be bound in heaven, and whatever you loose on earth will be loosed in heaven." (Matthew 16:18-19)

*

Remember Jesus Christ, raised from the dead, a descendant of David—that is my gospel, for which I suffer hardship, even to the point of being chained like a criminal. But the word of God is not chained. (2 Timothy 2:8-9)

*

Now many signs and wonders were done among the people through the apostles. And they were all together in Solomon's Portico. . . . A great number of people would also gather from the towns around Jerusalem, bringing the sick and those tormented by unclean spirits, and they were all cured.

Then the high priest took action; he and all who were with him (that is, the sect of the Sadducees), being filled with jealousy, arrested the apostles and put them in the public prison. But during the night an angel of the Lord opened the prison doors, brought them out, and said, "Go, stand in the temple and tell the people the whole message about this life." When they heard this, they entered the temple at daybreak and went on with their teaching.

When the high priest and those with him arrived, they called together the council and the whole body of the elders of Israel, and sent to the prison to have them brought. But when the temple police went there, they did not find them in the prison; so they returned and reported, "We found the prison securely locked and the guards standing at the doors, but when we opened them, we found no one inside." Now when the captain of the temple and the chief priests heard these words, they were perplexed about them, wondering what might be going on. Then someone arrived and announced, "Look, the men whom you put in prison are standing in the temple and teaching the people!" (Acts 5:12, 16-25)

*

"But woe to you, scribes and Pharisees, hypocrites! For you lock people out of the kingdom of heaven. For you do not go in yourselves, and when others are going in, you stop them." (Matthew 23:13)

*

On that day I will call my servant Eliakim son of Hilkiah, . . . I will place on his shoulder the key of the house of David; he shall open, and no one shall shut; he shall shut, and no one shall open. (Isaiah 22:20, 22)

Considering

Keys are both a practical necessity in our lives and also a powerful symbol. For example, even though these keys are just lying there, each one represents a great deal of activity and responsibility in your life. One way that we can see this symbolism at work is that whenever a visiting dignitary comes to town, we often give them a symbolic key to the city.

Keys are not new in human society; there were evidently keys even in ancient Egypt, and we know that keys were generally much larger until about a century and a half ago. Today, these small pieces of metal (or keyless remote controls) allow us access to parts of our lives we want to keep safe or private from others.

Although we may not stop to consider it very often, God is a part of every area of our lives; we can't "lock God out" of any part of who we are and what we do.

Responding

How do we make sure that God is "key" in our lives and that we don't try to "lock up" the word and the power of God by not trusting God enough or having specific ideas of what God should or should not be doing in our lives? Loving God, help me to "unlock" my heart and my life to let you into my life all the way, to be a part of all that I do and all that I am.

Keys: The Power of God

As I do that, help me to be careful of how I act and how I treat others, especially how I use my words to speak to them, as the book of Sirach reminds me: "As you fence in your property with thorns, so make a door and a bolt for your mouth. As you lock up your silver and gold, so make balances and scales for your words" (Sirach 28:24-25). Are there some specific ways in which I need to watch how I talk to or about others?

Loving God, you have the "key" to everlasting life and to my happiness with you; help me to be "open" to your love and to remember this when I use my keys. Amen.

Money: The Root of All Evil?

Materials at hand: Money—both coins and bills (and foreign money, if you have any), with a candle as a prayer focus.

Centering

(Light the candle and with your hands spread open say:)
Loving God, Creator of all that is,
here I am—today, in this place,
with all the senses you have given me.
Help me to use them to come to experience you more deeply.
You are present everywhere around me;
open me to know more of the many ways
that your goodness surrounds me.
Thank you for this time to be with you and to listen to you.
Amen.

Savoring

Look at the money before you as though you had never seen it before. It is strange, when you think of it, to use special pieces of paper and round pieces of metal to stand for a certain amount of value, whether of work or of goods. (If you've been to other countries and used their currency, this thought may have occurred to you in that situation.) Imagine, if you can, the stories each coin or bill could tell if it could speak, of where and when it has ended up changing hands and how that happened.

Try to anticipate the way the money will feel in your hand, especially if you have any foreign money that you don't often touch. Now hold the money, one piece at a time, with your eyes closed, noticing any small differences in texture that your eyes may have missed. For example, are there any ridges around the edges of any of these coins? What is the sound, if any, that the bills make as you fold or slightly crinkle them near your ear? Pick up all the money and let it fall to the table at once, listening to the sound it makes as it hits the table.

What does money *mean* to you? Those who study personal relationships tell us that disagreements over money within families are often really about the different meanings we attach to money. If you had to complete the sentence, "To me, money ultimately means . . . ," what would you say? Is it security, power, freedom—or what? We "spend" so much energy each day on gaining or using money, which is ultimately quite abstract!

Listening

Listen to and reflect on one or more of these passages as you watch the candlelight play across the money:

> [Jesus] sat down opposite the treasury, and watched the crowd putting money into the treasury. Many rich people put in large sums. A poor widow came and put in two small copper coins, which are worth a penny. Then he called his disciples and said to them, "Truly I tell you, this poor widow has put in more than all those who are contributing to the treasury. For all of them have contributed out of their abundance; but she out of her poverty has put in everything she had, all she had to live on." (Mark 12:41-44)
>
> *
>
> [The rich young man] said to [Jesus], "Teacher, I have kept all these [commandments] since my youth." Jesus, looking at him, loved him and said, "You lack one thing; go, sell what you own, and give the money to the poor, and you will have treasure in heaven; then come, follow me." When he heard this, he was shocked and went away grieving, for he had many possessions.
>
> Then Jesus looked around and said to his disciples, "How hard it will be for those who have wealth to enter the kingdom of God!" (Mark 10:20-23)
>
> *
>
> In the temple he found people selling cattle, sheep, and doves, and the money changers seated at their tables. Making a whip of cords,

he drove all of them out of the temple, both the sheep and the cattle. He also poured out the coins of the money changers and overturned their tables. He told those who were selling the doves, "Take these things out of here! Stop making my Father's house a marketplace!" (John 2:14-16)

*

Then the Pharisees went and plotted to entrap him in what he said. So they sent their disciples to him . . . saying, "Teacher . . . tell us . . . what you think. Is it lawful to pay taxes to the emperor, or not?" But Jesus, aware of their malice, said, "Why are you putting me to the test, you hypocrites? Show me the coin used for the tax." And they brought him a denarius. Then he said to them, "Whose head is this, and whose title?" They answered, "The emperor's." Then he said to them, "Give therefore to the emperor the things that are the emperor's, and to God the things that are God's." When they heard this, they were amazed; and they left him and went away. (Matthew 22:15-22)

*

"Do not store up for yourselves treasures on earth, where moth and rust consume and where thieves break in and steal; but store up for yourselves treasures in heaven, where neither moth nor rust consumes and where thieves do not break in and steal. For where your treasure is, there your heart will be also." (Matthew 6:19-21)

Considering

Money allows a society to work much more smoothly and to exchange goods and services better. Without it, there is only the barter system or a direct exchange economy, where the person with something to trade has to find someone who both wants it and has something acceptable to trade in return. Money allows a much greater flexibility for everyone.

Before paper and coins were used regularly as money, various societies used other substances, such as rice or small tools (China), cowrie shells (India), metal disks (Tibet), dog's teeth (Papua New Guinea), quartz pebbles (Ghana), and limestone disks (Yap Island). Paper money was first used in China, probably around 600 A.D., although it wasn't used in Europe until the 1600s and was issued only by banks or private companies until finally issued by governments in the 1800s. Playing cards signed by the French

Canadian colonial governor were even used as money for a while in the late seventeenth and early eighteenth centuries because of a shortage of cash!

As contemporary money has gotten further away from a gold or silver standard—with those metals on hand in the treasury to back up its worth—and as more currency is exchanged and transferred electronically, money seems to be becoming an increasingly important symbol of international trust.

Responding

Money and the ways we manage it can connect with our faith and spirituality, even though it may not seem so at first. For one thing, the way we use our money is a powerful indication of our *true* values, not just what we *say* is important.

Money can also distract us spiritually; St. Paul warns about some of the dangers associated with it in his letter to Timothy in a passage that is often misquoted:

> But those who want to be rich fall into temptation and are trapped by many senseless and harmful desires that plunge people into ruin and destruction. For the love of money is a root of all kinds of evil, and in their eagerness to be rich some have wandered away from the faith and pierced themselves with many pains. (1 Timothy 6:9-10)

It is *the love of money*, not money itself, that Paul says is the root of many evils. If we're not careful, money and its pursuit can derail us from what is really important in life, things we know money can't buy. Scripture is full of references to God's special love for the poor, not because money is bad but because those who are poor are aware of how much they really need God. Scripture also talks often about almsgiving, or generosity to the poor. Do I tithe (give ten percent or at least a certain part) of my time or income to help those who may not have all that I do? And do I let what I have or want to have keep me from realizing that God is what I really need?

Loving God of all that is truly valuable, help those without enough money to live safely and with some comfort. Bless those who work with the poor as well as those who work with money in banks, mints, financial institutions, or retail or wholesale sales; help them to be fair and honest as they deal with others and with money.

Bless those in the poorer countries of the world whose indebtedness to the wealthier countries and the interest they owe may hinder them from helping their own people. Bless also those who gamble with their money not to be controlled by their games. And help me to remember when I'm feeling pressured to buy and spend because I really "need" what is being sold that it is your love that really has "value" in my life. Amen.

. . . And More

If you'd like to continue praying with a hands-on approach, try to be specifically aware each day of one sight, sound, smell, taste, or touch so that at the end of the day you can ask yourself what your senses remember from the day. Recall that sense experience and be thankful for God's presence in it and for all the other ways that God was there that you weren't as aware of.

Be grateful for the sense you used in that situation and for all your senses and for those who have helped you know God more deeply in your day and in your life, and ask for the grace to be open to God's presence more fully tomorrow.

Don't forget to end with "Amen," for it is true.

For Further Reading

The following books may help you continue to see the everyday objects around you as holy:

Sue Bender, *Plain and Simple: A Woman's Journey to the Amish* (Harper & Row, 1989) and *Everyday Sacred: A Woman's Journey Home* (HarperSanFrancisco, 1995).

Using simple objects like Amish quilts and begging bowls, Sue Bender encourages us to look again at the everyday stuff of life.

*

Mark G. Boyer, *Home Is a Holy Place: Reflections, Prayers and Meditations Inspired by the Ordinary* (ACTA Publications, 1997).

Short reflections on everything from an apron to a zipper.

*

Gunilla Norris, *Being Home: A Book of Meditations* (Bell Tower, 1991).

The author takes us through a typical day, exploring the holiness of activities such as paying bills and arranging flowers in the course of her simple meditations.

*

Joyce Rupp, *The Cup of Our Life: A Guide for Spiritual Growth* (Ave Maria Press, 1997).

This wonderful book includes six weeks' worth of meditations on our lives as we pray with a simple cup. This resource can be used individually or in a group.